FOREWORD TO THE 1991 CENTENARY EDITION

In this year when Theosophists throughout the world will be remembering with gratitude the life and work of Madame Blavatsky, Co-Founder of the Theosophical Society, it has been thought desirable to make available to the present generation of Theosophical students the tributes offered to her memory by some of those who were closest to her in her later years. These memorial articles were first published in the magazine *Lucifer* shortly after Madame Blavatsky's death in May 1891, and appeared in book form later in the same year.

In 1931, in honour of the Centenary of Madame Blavatsky's birth, an edition was published by the Blavatsky Association of London, with several photographs and some additional items. In this facsimile edition of the original volume, only the frontispiece photograph and this brief note have been added.

MAGNA EST VERITAS ET PRAEVALEBIT

The Theosophical Publishing House Ltd., London

1991

ISBN 07229 1003 7

The Theosophical Publishing House Ltd.
12 Bury Place, London WC1A 2LE

HELENA PETROVNA BLAVATSKY

H. P. B.

In Memory of

HELENA PETROVNA BLAVATSKY

BY

SOME OF HER PUPILS

London:

THEOSOPHICAL PUBLISHING SOCIETY, 7, Duke Street, Adelphi, W.C.

New York: The *Path* Office, 132, Nassau Street.

Madras: Theosophical Headquarters, Adyar.

1891

———

PRICE ONE SHILLING.

LONDON :
WOMEN'S PRINTING SOCIETY, LIMITED,
GREAT COLLEGE STREET, WESTMINSTER, S.W.

H. P. B.

Elle vécut dans l' angoisse, et mourut dans le travail ;
mais elle eut de la gloire, et elle fut aimée.

How she left us.

IT having been my privilege to be with H. P. B. during her last illness, and at the moment of her death, I have been asked to contribute my share to the "Memories" which have been written for the benefit of the brother and sister Theosophists, who being far away have not had the advantage of seeing and being with H. P. B. constantly.

It was on Tuesday, the 21st of April, that I went to stay at Headquarters for the few days, which, owing to the unexpected events that followed, turned into a visit of some weeks. H. P. B. seemed in her usual state of health, and on Thursday, the 23rd, attended the Lodge and remained chatting with the friends who surrounded her for some time after the proceedings of the evening were over ; she then adjourned to her room where, according to their habit, members who live at Headquarters followed to sit with her while she took her coffee before retiring for the night. The following day, Friday, passed quietly over, giving no warning that a fortnight from that date our beloved H. P. B. would leave us. The next evening, Saturday, she was very bright. Dr. Mennell called and was perfectly satisfied with her condition. My sister, Mrs. Cooper-Oakley, and I, with one or two others, remained talking with her until eleven o'clock, when she retired with a cheery " Good night all ", apparently in her usual health. The next morning, however, H. P. B.'s maid came early to my room to tell me she had passed a very restless night and had been seized with shivering attacks. I went down shortly-after, and the first glance shewed me that she was evidently in a high state of fever. The doctor was immediately sent for, and the day passed with H. P. B. alternately in a heavy sleep, or in a state of restlessness. Late in the afternoon Dr. Mennell came, pronounced the illness to be influenza ; the fever was very high, her temperature being 105. Fearing the probable complications which might ensue owing to H. P. B.'s chronic illness, Dr. Mennell at once took a serious view of her case and said she must have with her, during the night, a responsible member of the household in addition to her maid, it being of the utmost importance that both medicine and food should be given punctually. The duty fell on me, for the Countess Wachtmeister being engaged in business all day could not sit up during the night, and my sister was not permitted by Dr. Mennell to do so, owing to the fact that in addition to being engaged in business she had recently been very ill.

From that memorable Sunday night, April 26th, began the succession of misfortunes, the illness of one member of the household after another, which culminated in the passing away of our beloved H. P. B. The hours slowly passed in alternations of restlessness and sleep, and with the morning came little or no change for the better. H. P. B. had her large armchair brought from her sitting room and placed by her bed, that she might be able to gain a little ease by changing from one position to another. Though feeling very ill she asked to be told all that was going on, and was concerned on hearing that another member, Mr. Sturdy, had also been taken ill with influenza ; when it was suggested that Mr. Mead should bring him to be nursed at Headquarters, she was much pleased and insisted on his being sent for at once.

H. P. B. spent a most suffering day, and when Dr. Mennell came early in the evening he was distressed to find the fever was still very high ; he changed the medicine, giving a preparation of salycene, it being absolutely necessary to reduce the temperature, and decided to call again about midnight to see the result ; he left strict orders that before each dose the temperature should be carefully taken, for in the event of a sudden fall taking place it would have been dangerous to continue the medicine. Before he came again that night a third dose fell due, but owing to the decrease in H. P. B.'s temperature, I felt justified in not giving it, especially as the discomforts incidental to the drug were beginning to cause her much uneasiness. And it was a relief, when Dr. Mennell came, to find the right course had been taken, for he was satisfied with her condition. She passed a fairly quiet night, and on Tuesday morning the fever had almost gone ; that day and the following night all seemed going on well, for though the weakness was very distressing, no complications had as yet appeared, and she was able to take plenty of nourishment. Towards the end of Thursday the 30th, H. P. B. began to suffer very much from her throat, and as the hours went by she had increasing difficulty in swallowing ; her cough became very troublesome and her breathing very laboured. On Friday morning she was no better, and when Dr. Mennell arrived he found a quinsy had formed in the right side of the throat ; hot poultices were applied and some relief was gained. During the evening the quinsy broke, and when Dr. Mennell came again he was comparatively satisfied with H. P. B.'s condition. The improvement, however, was not of long duration ; a bad night followed, and in the morning it became apparent there was a second formation in the throat. This proved to be an abscess on the bronchial tube. A wretched day and night succeeded and the morning of Sunday, May 3rd, found H. P. B. very ill indeed, for the pain of swallowing made it very difficult for her to take the necessary amount of nourishment, and her weakness increased in consequence. Monday and Tuesday passed in much the same manner; the abscess disappeared, but the bronchial tubes being much affected, the difficulty in breathing still continued, and almost constant fanning had to be kept up to relieve the dreadful oppression from which she was suffering. How bravely she struggled against her illness only those who were with her can realise. On Wednesday, the 6th May, she partially dressed and walked into the sitting-room, remained there for her luncheon, resting for some time on the sofa; in the evening Dr. Mennell found her going on fairly well, all fever had entirely left her, but the great weakness and the difficulty in breathing caused him considerable anxiety. Several times H.P.B. told Dr. Mennell she felt she was dying, and that she could not keep up the struggle much longer; but he, knowing the illnesses she had previously conquered, did not give up hope; indeed, I may say this feeling was shared throughout the house, for though we realized how seriously ill H.P.B. was, we could not believe she would leave us.

One bad symptom was that from the first days of her illness, H.P.B. lost all desire for smoking her cigarettes, and though, when the fever left her, she tried to begin again it gave her no pleasure and she finally threw up the attempt. It had always been her custom to roll a few cigarettes for Dr. Mennell when he called, and all through her illness she never failed to have some ready; sometimes in the course of the morning, with many a pause, she would succeed in rolling one or two, and later when she became too weak to roll the cigarettes herself either Mr. Mead or Mr. Wright was called for that purpose. That Wednesday night was the turning point in her illness; about midnight a change for the worse took place and for an hour or two it seemed as if H.P.B. must go; she had no perceptible pulse, and it seemed almost impossible for her to get breath. After a time the attack passed off; she became a little easier, and for the time the danger passed. Very early on Thursday morning Mr. Wright went for Dr. Mennell, who returned with him and remained for some time to watch the effect of the medicine he gave—during the day H.P.B. rallied and about three in the afternoon dressed, and with very little assistance walked into the sitting room; when there she asked for her large armchair to be brought her and while it was being placed in its old position near her writing table, she stood merely leaning slightly against the table. The chair was turned facing into the room and when H.P.B. was sitting in it she had her card table with the cards drawn in front of her, and she tried to "make a patience"; notwithstanding all these brave efforts it was quite apparent that she was suffering intensely, and that nothing but her powerful will could have sustained her in the struggle; the intense difficulty in breathing had brought a strained pathetic expression into H.P.B.'s dear face most pitiful to see, and it seemed to show even more when she attempted any return to her old habits. Dr. Mennell came shortly after 5 o'clock

and was much surprised to find her sitting up, and he congratulated
her and praised her courage; she said, "I do my best, Doctor"; her
voice was hardly above a whisper and the effort to speak was exhaust-
ing, as her breath was very short, but she was less deaf and liked to
hear conversation. She handed Dr. Mennell a cigarette she had managed
with difficulty to prepare for him; it was the last she ever made. After a
little time Dr. Mennell asked H.P.B. if she would mind seeing his partner
Dr. Miller, and allowing him to listen to her chest; she consented, he came
in at once, and the examination took place; a consultation was held, and
then Dr. Mennell called Mrs. Oakley and myself to hear Dr. Miller's
opinion. He considered H.P.B.'s condition very serious, owing to the
bronchitis from which she was suffering and her extreme weakness; he
advised a tablespoonful of brandy every two hours, the quantity to be
increased if necessary. This change in the treatment was at once made,
and it seemed to produce a good effect. Shortly after Dr. Mennell left
H.P.B. returned to her bedroom and her chair was once again placed
beside her bed; she was very tired, but asked as usual after the other
invalids, particularly wishing to know if there was a good Lodge Meeting.
The night that followed, her last with us, was a very suffering one; owing
to the increased difficulty in breathing H.P.B. could not rest in any
position; every remedy was tried without avail, and finally she was obliged
to remain seated in her chair propped with pillows. The cough almost
ceased, owing to her great exhaustion, though she had taken both medicine
and stimulant with regularity. About 4 a.m. H.P.B. seemed easier, and
her pulse was fairly strong, and from that time until I left her at 7 o'clock
all went quietly and well. My sister then took my place, while I went for
a few hours' rest, leaving word for Dr. Mennell to give me his opinion of
H.P.B. when he called. This he did shortly after nine, and his report was
satisfactory; the stimulant was having a good effect and the pulse stronger;
he saw no cause for immediate anxiety, advised me to rest a few hours,
and told my sister she could go to her business. About 11.30 I was aroused
by Mr. Wright, who told me to come at once as H.P.B. had changed for
the worse, and the nurse did not think she could live many hours; directly
I entered her room I realised the critical condition she was in. She was
sitting in her chair and I knelt in front of her and asked her to try and take
the stimulant; though too weak to hold the glass herself she allowed me to hold
it to her lips, and she managed to swallow the contents; but after that we
could only give a little nourishment in a spoon. The nurse said H.P.B.
might linger some hours, but suddenly there was a further change, and when
I tried to moisten her lips I saw the dear eyes were already becoming dim,
though she retained full consciousness to the last. In life H.P.B. had a
habit of moving one foot when she was thinking intently, and she continued
that movement almost to the moment she ceased to breathe. When all
hope was over the nurse left the room, leaving C. F. Wright, W. R. Old

and myself with our beloved H.P.B.; the two former knelt in front, each holding one of her hands, and I at her side with one arm round her supported her head; thus we remained motionless for many minutes, and so quietly did H.P.B. pass away that we hardly knew the second she ceased to breathe; a great sense of peace filled the room, and we knelt quietly there until, first my sister, then the Countess arrived. I had telegraphed to them and Dr. Mennell when the nurse said the end was near, but they were not in time to see H.P.B. before she left us. No time was lost in vain regrets, we all tried to think and to do what she would have wished under the circumstances, and we could only be thankful she was released from her suffering. The one ray of light in the darkness of our loss seems to be, that had there not been the instruments in the Society to carry on the work she would not have left us. She has bequeathed to us all as legacy the care of the Society she founded, the service of the cause to which her life was given, and the depth of our love and our loyalty will be measured by the strenuousness of our work.

LAURA M. COOPER, F.T.S.

The Cremation.

THE quiet of Headquarters early on Monday morning, May 11th, was remarkable. There was no hurry, nothing to show that anything unusual was to take place, except the serious faces of the residents and the constant receipts of telegrams. Shortly before 10 a number of Theosophists arrived, and together with those of the staff who had not the immediate direction of affairs, stood waiting in a double line in the hall and covered way. With quiet order the transfer was duly effected and the simple hearse started for Waterloo Station, accompanied by three members, the others finding their way to the station as they pleased, it being the repeatedly expressed wish of H.P.B. that no show or parade of any kind should be made over her body.

At Waterloo were many familiar faces, though not so many as there would have been had the notice been longer, as the many letters of regret for enforced absence testified. To an outsider who did not understand the spirit that animated the assembled Theosophists, and who had never regarded death as a mere change and the body as simply a garment, the absence of all mourning and the usual funeral paraphernalia must have caused some surprise. But to all of us present there seemed an appropriateness in making the last act in the drama of so unconventional a life in harmony with the rest.

The way from the Woking station to the Crematorium led through a length of pleasant sunlit lanes, arched over with new-born leaves, and the beauty of a glorious May morning brightened the grief which even the calmest-minded felt, for it takes many incarnations to " kill the heart " and lose all preference for the personality. Indeed on that particular morning nature showed herself in one of her happiest moods and seemed to smile a joyous farewell to the body of one of her dearest and most wondrously endowed children.

The Officers of the Society and the Headquarters Staff surrounded the flower-decked bier, and all remained in deepest silence while G. R. S. Mead, the General Secretary of the European Section, and Private Secretary to H.P.B. for the past two years, standing at the head, read the following address :—

FRIENDS AND BROTHER THEOSOPHISTS,

H. P. Blavatsky is dead, but H.P.B., our teacher and friend, is alive, and will live forever in our hearts and memories. In our present sorrow, it is this thought especially that we should keep ever before our minds. It is true that the personality we know as H. P. Blavatsky will be with us no longer ; but it is equally true that the grand and noble individuality, the great soul that has taught all of us men and women to live purer and more unselfish lives, is still active.

The Theosophical Society, which was her great work in this incarnation, still continues under the care and direction of those great living Masters and Teachers whose messenger she was, and whose work she will resume amongst us at no distant period.

Dear as the personality of H.P.B. is to us, to many of whom she took the place of a dearly loved and reverenced mother, still we must remember that, as she has so often taught us, the personality is the impermanent part of man's nature and the mere outer dress of the real individuality.

The real H.P.B. does not lie here before us. The true self that inspired so many men and women in every quarter of the earth with a noble enthusiasm for suffering humanity and the true progress of the race, combined with a lofty ideal of individual life and conduct, can in the mind of no Theosophist be confounded with the mere physical instrument which served it for one brief incarnation.

Fellow Theosophists, the duty that lies before us, her pupils and friends, is plain and simple. As we all know so well, the one great purpose of our teacher's life in this her present incarnation, a purpose which she pursued with such complete unselfishness and singleness of. motive, was to restore to mankind the knowledge of those great spiritual truths we to-day call Theosophy.

Her unvarying fidelity to her great mission, from which neither contumely nor misrepresentation ever made her swerve, was the key-note of her strong and fearless nature. To her who knew so well its true and inner meaning, Theosophy was an ever-present power in her life, and she was ceaseless in her endeavours to spread the knowledge of the living truths of which she had such full assurance, so that by their ever-widening influence the wave of materiality in Science and Religion might be checked, and a real and lasting spiritual foundation laid for the true progress and brotherhood of mankind.

With such an example before us, then, our duty as Theosophists is clear. We must continue the work that H.P.B. has so nobly commenced, if not with her power—which to us is as yet impossible—at least with an enthusiasm, self-sacrifice and determination such as alone can show our gratitude to her and our appreciation of the great task she has committed to us.

We must, therefore, each individually take up our share of that task. Theosophy is not dead because to-day we stand by H. P. B.'s dead body. It lives and must live, because Truth can never die ; but on us, the up-holders of this Truth, must ever rest the heaviest of all responsibilities, the effort so to shape our own characters and lives that that truth may be there-by commended to others.

Most fortunately for all of us, H. P. B. leaves the work on a firm foun-dation and fully organized. In spite of failing health and bodily pain, our beloved leader to the very last moments of her life continued her unceasing exertions for the cause we all love so well. Never did she relax one moment from her vigilance over its interests, and she repeatedly impressed upon those who surrounded her the principles and methods by which the work was to be carried on, never contemplating for one instant that the death of her body could be any real hindrance to the performance of the duty which would then more than ever be incumbent on every earnest member of the Society. This duty, which lies so clearly before us, and of which H. P. B. has set us so striking an example, is to spread the know-ledge of Theosophy by every means in our power, especially by the influence of our own lives.

Much as we love and reverence our leader, our devotion to the work must not rest on the transient basis of affection for a personality, but on the solid foundation of a conviction that in Theosophy itself, and in it alone, are to be found those eternal spiritual principles of right thought, right speech and right action, which are essential to the progress and harmony of mankind.

We believe that if H. P. B. could stand here in the body and speak to us now, this would be her message to all the members of the Theosophical Society, not simply to those who are present, but to all who without dis-tinction of race, creed, or sex, are with us in heart and sympathy to-day. She would tell us as she has told many of us already, that a "clean life, an open mind, a pure heart, an eager intellect, an unveiled spiritual percep-tion, a brotherliness for all, a readiness to give and receive advice and in-struction, a courageous endurance of personal injustice, a brave declaration of principles, a valiant defence of those who are unjustly attacked, and a constant eye to the ideal of human progression and perfection which the Sacred Science depicts—these are the golden stairs up the steps of which the learner may climb to the Temple of Divine Wisdom."

And now in silence we leave the body of our teacher and go back to the every-day world. In our hearts we shall ever carry with us her memory, her example, her life. Every Theosophical truth that we utter, every Theosophical effort that we make, is one more evidence of our love for her, and what should be greater even than that, of our devotion to the cause for which she lived. To that cause she was ever true—to that truth let none of us be ever false.

A brief silence succeeded, and then the vehicle that bore the body of the greatest of the Theosophists passed through the folding doors of the Crematorium. Nothing could have been simpler. No ceremony, no pomp or pageantry, no distressing signs of emotion or useless mourning ; and yet the last act of honour to our great leader's body was far from being without its impressiveness ; and the scene at Woking will ever live in the memories of the spectators, who could not fail to sense the grave seriousness of the occasion, the deep and suppressed feelings of the mourners, and the determination shown in the set faces of those who work for Theosophy.

Two hours afterwards the urn containing the ashes of our beloved teacher's body was reverently received, and carried back to Headquarters and placed in her own rooms, thus terminating a very eventful day for the Theosophic world.

Yes ; that last farewell to H. P. B.'s recent garment of flesh marks an important epoch in the annals of the Theosophical Society, and a new point of departure for increased effort and exertion.

In the hearts of those who are endeavouring to make Theosophy a real factor in their lives, there must remain an overwhelming sense of gratitude to her who has inspired them with the will to do so ; and this sense of gratitude, love and respect will never be content until it can find fit expression. No material memorial, nothing that money can purchase, will ever be judged a sufficient tribute to her memory. There is but one way in which the debt can be paid, and that is by making the Theosophical Society a world-wide success and Theosophy known throughout the whole globe. The work to be done is one not only of head and hands but also of heart, the well-spring of all right actions and the real magnet-point of our humanity. The tremendous burden of responsibility that lay so heavily on H. P. B., but which she so gladly bore for the Society, must now be shared among ourselves. No longer can H. P. B. stand as a " buffer ", as she herself phrased it, to the Society and be the scape-goat of all its short-comings. While she lived, every mistake and wrong-doing of those who surrounded her were set down to H. P. B. and she had to bear the blame for all. This is now no longer possible. The Theosophical

Society and each of its members must stand upon their own merits, and the day of vicarious atonement is past. If the world is to respect Theosophy, we must make it first of all respect the Theosophical Society, both for its labours for others and for the immediate good it does to those who come within its pale. We must teach and exemplify : teach what Theosophy is in plain and simple words, and exemplify its redeeming power by our right conduct in all the affairs of life.

He alone is a true Theosophist who develops all his higher faculties and learns to sense the " fitness of things ", their underlying harmony, on all occasions. Right thought, right feeling, right speech, right judgment and right action are the signs of such an one, and will indubitably lead to that consummation of brotherhood which we have before us as our ideal.

Let us, then, who would fairly earn the title of Theosophist, see well to this and follow the example of H. P. B. in sacrificing ourselves for the good of others.

" As a mother, even at the risk of her own life, protects her son, her only son : so let there be goodwill without measure among all beings. Let goodwill without measure prevail in the whole world, above, below, around, unstinted, unmixed with any feeling of differing or opposing interests. If a man remain steadfastly in this state of mind all the while he is awake, whether he be standing, walking, sitting, or lying down, then is come to pass the saying ' even in this world happiness has been found '."*

G. R. S. MEAD, F.T.S.

———✳———

At New York and Würzburg.

MY earliest acquaintance with H. P. B. dates from the autumn of the year 1877, when I took advantage of a three months' leave of absence from my duties in England to seek her out in New York. The Spiritualist movement, with which I was officially connected, was at that time in full swing, and the appearance of Col. Olcott's book, *People from Another World*, was making a great stir, chiefly on account of the strange occurrences therein reported as taking place in Vermont, through the mediumship of the Eddy brothers. The part of the book which attracted me however, was that in which Col. Olcott related the appearance on the scene of the Russian lady lately arrived from the East, and whose explanation of the phenomena was widely different from that generally received. As soon as I learned the address of Madame Blavatsky from the American Spiritualist journals, I wrote to her, and it was in consequence of our correspondence that I was induced to visit America.

Our first introduction was a singular one. I was staying at some distance from West 34th Street, where H. P. B. was then residing, and

---

* *Metta Sutta* quoted in Rhys David's " Buddhism ".

one afternoon, soon after my arrival, I went to call on her. After ringing three times in vain, I was about to turn away in despair, when the door was opened by H. P. B. herself! Having already exchanged photographs, recognition was mutual, and my welcome the heartiest imaginable. We went up to the flat on the second floor, and who that has ever known H. P. B. will fail to understand how hospitable was her reception, and how when Col. Olcott returned from the City, I was already quite at home. I could not remain then, for I was leaving New York the next day on a little tour to Niagara and elsewhere; but on my return three weeks later, I spent five weeks with H. P. B., until I finally left for England.

Just at that time *Isis Unveiled* was going through the press, and many were the happy hours I spent correcting proof-sheets and discussing the problems put forward in that marvellous book. These are personal details and seem too trivial to be recorded; yet how lovingly does the mind linger round the smallest incident, and try to recall, in the light of after events, the *minutiæ* of those precious opportunities, too little valued at the time! While the intellectual work was going on, and details connected with printing and publishing had to be attended to, there were perhaps fewer of the so-called " phenomena " which were frequent in those early days of the Theosophical Society; but what phenomenon could well be greater than the production of H. P. B.'s monumental works, in a language and country foreign to her, unless it were the union in one individual of such great knowledge, such spiritual wealth, with so much geniality and consideration for the meanest brother or sister who showed aspiration for truth or goodness, so much sympathy and ready help in difficulties of every kind, material as well as psychical and spiritual.

When I consider how few of the teachings of Theosophy as since given to the world were then unfolded, I am amazed to think how one mind could contain them all without making them known. But the time had not yet come. The encounter in those days was largely with those who were engaged in the investigation of modern spiritualism, as the pages of *Isis* plainly show, and it was some years before the world, even the world to whom Madame Blavatsky's writings chiefly appealed, was aware of the full brilliance of that meteor which had shot from the Eastern across the Western sky. How many more years will yet elapse before a tithe of her teachings become common property? We shall see. The charm of her personal presence, her brilliant conversation, her sallies of wit and humour, her infinite variety which no custom could ever stale, never failed from the first to draw around her endless numbers of visitors and acquaintances, besides the friends who knew something of her real worth. But it was only those who lived with her constantly, or for any length of time together, and who had occasional glimpses of the real self behind the fluctuating exterior, who could know how true and large, how generous and noble was the heart that beat within.

Various instances of H. P. B.'s psychical powers occurred while I was with her, but most of these are difficult to record, are in fact incommunicable. The following is, however, patent to all:—One morning at breakfast she told us that she had while asleep seen her nephew killed in the war then going on between Russia and Turkey. She described the manner of his death-blow, how he was wounded, the fall from his horse and other details. She requested Col. Olcott and myself to make a note of it, as well as the date, and before I left New York full confirmation of the event was received in a letter from Russia, all the circumstances corresponding with H. P. B's. dream or vision. Duplication of objects was not uncommonly practised by H. P. B. at that period, and occurred both in my own presence and in that of persons on whose testimony I could perfectly rely.

It required no special insight to perceive that communication was constantly kept up with some distant or invisible minds. Frequent signals of various kinds were heard even at the dinner-table, when H. P. B. would immediately retire to her own apartment. So familiar were these sounds as well as the terms "Masters", and "Brothers", that when in after years so much controversy as to their reality took place, even among those calling themselves Theosophists, it never occurred to me to doubt their existence.

At this time attacks on H. P. B.'s writings and personal character were rife in the American journals, and on my return to England I had to encounter almost single-handed the opposition of the English Spiritualists, on account of her explanations of their favourite "manifestations". Finally I left both the Spiritualist and Theosophical Societies, and did not see Madame Blavatsky again for many years; yet so strong and ineffaceable was the impression produced on my mind by her nobleness of character, her truthfulness and honesty, that no sooner had I heard of the Report of the Psychical Society, than I determined to go to H. P. B., if anywhere within reach, if only as a silent protest against the action of those most unfair and mis-guided gentlemen, who had endorsed so foul a slander. I found her at Würzburg with the Countess Wachtmeister, writing the *Secret Doctrine*, and from that time till H. P. B.'s death our connection has become ever closer and more binding.

If these few lines appear egotistical to the reader, I can only ask what tribute to the power of spirit can be greater than the declaration that in spite of every adverse influence being brought to bear, hers in the end became paramount, and is destined to sway those who came under its influence to the end of time.

Each can only speak as he or she has been personally affected; and such egotism, if egotism it be, is but a triumphant verdict in favour of her we fain would honour, whose greatest glory was the number of hearts and minds she won for the pursuit of truth and virtue.

EMILY KISLINGBURY.

At Cairo and Madras.

IMPOSSIBLE is it for me, in the short space allotted, to give any details of the many deeply interesting times I have spent with our beloved Teacher and leader : I will therefore confine myself to the memorable winter of 1884-85, when the much-talked-of Coulomb affair took place. It was, without doubt, a momentous crisis in the history of the Theosophical movement of this century ; and being thus important, details given by an eye-witness may be of interest.

H. P. B. had been staying during the summer with Miss Arundale in Elgin Crescent, but left her house to join Mr. Oakley and myself, and remained with us until we started for India with her. The house party consisted of H. P. B., my sister, Dr. Keightley, Mr. Oakley and myself. It was early in November, 1884, that we left Liverpool for Port Said *en route* for Madras. It had been arranged that we were to go first to Cairo in order to get some definite information about the antecedents of the Coulombs, who were well known there, as the news of their treachery had already reached us some months before, news which H. P. B. had taken very calmly. We reached Port Said on the 17th of November, 1884, and there remained some few days for Mr. Leadbeater to join us ; on his arrival we took the mail boat down the Suez Canal to Ismailia, and then went by train to Cairo. Very deeply impressed on my memory is every incident connected with that memorable voyage. H. P. B. was a most interesting fellow-traveller, her varied information about every part of Egypt was both extensive and extraordinary. Would that I had space to go into the details of that time in Cairo, the drives through the quaint and picturesque bazaars, and her descriptions of the people and their ways. Especially interesting was one long afternoon spent at the Boulak Museum on the borders of the Nile, where H. P. B. astonished Maspero, the well-known Egyptologist, with her knowledge, and as we went through the museum she pointed out to him the grades of the Initiate kings, and how they were to be known from the esoteric side. But I must not linger over these memories of her.

To run briefly over events, H. P. B. and Colonel Olcott came to London from New York in 1878, and after a brief stay in England proceeded to Bombay where, at Girgaum, they opened the first Theosophical Headquarters in India and started the *Theosophist*. Soon after landing in Bombay, Madame Coulomb, who had once nursed H. P. B. in Cairo, appeared at Headquarters and appealed for assistance. It marks one of the strongest traits in our Teacher's character that she never forgot a kindness, however trivial and however unworthy the person who did it. So when Coulomb, with her husband, came half-starved and penniless to H. P. B., they were taken into shelter. Madame Coulomb was made housekeeper and Alexis Coulomb general manager, as there was a lack of competent help for household work. M. Coulomb was by trade a carpenter and mechanic.

In 1883 Colonel Olcott and H. P. B. made arrangements to visit Europe, and the Society's general affairs were turned over to a " Board of Control", the Coulombs having charge of the house and remaining especially upstairs, where H. P. B. used to live. No sooner had H. P. B. sailed than the Coulombs shut themselves away in the upper part of the house, which had a separate stair-case, and then Alexis Coulomb had over six months in which to do all his carpentering work, to make various trap doors and sliding panels for use in his conspiracy. They then proceeded to the missionaries in Madras, and offered to show them that tricks had been done, and they were paid by the missionaries for their pretended disclosures. Their plans were a.little hurried at the end, owing to the unexpected arrival of Mr. William Q. Judge from New York, and the decision of the Board of Control to discharge Coulomb. The rough and unfinished condition of the trap doors is accounted for by their hurried departure. The Rev. Mr. Patterson himself informed Mr. Judge of the payment that had been made to the Coulombs.

Thus far their history; now to return to our journey. On leaving Cairo, H. P. B. and I went straight to Suez. Mr. Oakley remained at Cairo to get the documents from the police about the Coulombs; Mr. Leadbeater joined us at Suez. After waiting two days for the steamer we started for Madras. I am not often thoroughly ashamed of my country men and women; but I confess I had reason to be so during that fortnight; the first pamphlets written by the missionaries were being circulated on board ship, and every insulting remark that could be made about H. P. B. was heard. That voyage was very unpleasant, but some few kindly incidents relieved the general monotony of incivility to our dear friend. Col. Olcott and some members met us at Colombo, and we stayed there nearly two days, paying some deeply interesting visits to the old Buddhist Temples, and one especially charming visit to Sumangala, the High Priest, who evidently had a very high respect for H. P. B. We then proceeded to Madras. Never shall I forget the quaint picturesqueness of our arrival there. A deputation, accompanied by a brass band, came off in boats to meet us; but the sound of the music was somewhat marred by the fact that the drop between the waves is so great that sometimes our band was on the top of a high roller, and sometimes almost engulfed between two big waves. On landing at the pier head there were hundreds to meet H. P. B., and we were literally towed by enthusiastic members down the pier in a truck, wildly decorated with paper roses, etc., and then surrounded by masses of smiling dark faces. She was driven off to Pacheappah's hall, where we had garlands of pink roses festooned round us, and were sprinkled somewhat copiously with rose water. Then H. P. B. and I were conducted by a Rajah to his carriage and driven off to Adyar. Here the warmest welcome awaited her. Members were assembling from all parts of India for the approaching Convention; we went into the large hall and at once began discussing the all-absorbing Coulomb case. Col. Olcott then informed us that the Society for Psychical Research was sending out a member to investigate the matter, and accordingly a few days after, the notorious Mr. Hodgson arrived fresh from Cambridge. And now a word on this young man. Mr. Hodgson was an Australian by birth, and came to England to make his way in the world, and being an enterprising young man he was willing to do anything with that end in view. I am quite confident that if an older man had come, one with more experience and a maturer judgment, the Coulomb affair would have been presented to the world in a very different way. It takes a cool head and a just nature to side with the minority, and when Mr. Hodgson arrived in India, he found the whole Anglo-Indian Community in arms against Madame Blavatsky on two principal points—(1) that she was a Russian spy, (2) that she sided with the Hindoos against Anglo-Indians, if she thought that the former were unjustly treated, and above all had the courage to say so. Now, the position of a young man who wanted at once to do the right thing and to be popular with the majority, was necessarily very difficult; and a continuous round of dinner parties did not tend to clear his views, for he had incessantly poured into his ears a stream of calumny against her. The general community hated her for the reasons I have given; and the Missionaries hated her because she was unorthodox and a Theosophist. Mr. Hodgson's investigations were not conducted with an unbiassed mind, and from hearing everyone say Madame Blavatsky was an impostor he began to believe it: after a few interviews with Madame Coulomb and the Missionaries we saw that his views were turning against the minority. Now his report was not by any means accurate, for he omitted some very valuable evidence of phenomena given to him by Mr. Oakley and myself. Mr. Hodgson was treated with the greatest courtesy and friendliness by H. P. B. and Col. Olcott, and every opportunity was afforded him for investigating every hole and corner at Adyar; and yet he preferred, and gave more credence to, the testimony of a discharged servant, whose bad character was by that time universally known, than to that of H. P. B. and her friends, who had no monetary interest in giving their evidence. The trap doors and sliding panels had all been made by Coulomb, in H. P. B.'s absence, and his wife sold the character of the mistress who had saved her from starvation to the Missionaries and forged the letters she showed to them. Any person of ordinary intellect and common sense could see that the trap doors and sliding panels were quite new, so new as to be immovable, *the grooves being quite fresh and unmarked by any* usage whatever, as Mr. Oakley and I found when we tried to move the largest sliding door. If we could not do so with our combined efforts, surely it is ridiculous to think Madame Blavatsky could have used them for conjuring tricks; the arrangements were so bad that any trick would have been inevitably discovered. However Mr. Hodgson was so bent on being a "success" that these simple common-sense facts were disregarded by him. Immediately after the convention was over he left Headquarters, and went to live in Madras, until his investigations were ended. How often did H. P. B. ask him to let her see the letters she was supposed to have written, but neither she, nor any of her intimate friends, were ever allowed to see them. No one who was not on the spot at the time could imagine the scandalous injustice with which she was treated. The effect of all this worry was that she became seriously ill. Col. Olcott had started for Burmah, Mr. Oakley and I were comparatively alone with her. Very anxious were the hours and days of nursing that I went through those three weeks, as she grew worse and worse and was finally given up in a state of coma by the doctors. It proves how wonderful was the protective influence of H. P. B., ill or well; for though I was completely isolated with her near the roof of the house, an open staircase leading up, hardly a soul within call, yet night after night have I wandered up and down the flat roof, to get a breath of fresh air between 3 and 4 a.m., and wondered as I watched the daylight break over the Bay of Bengal, why I felt so fearless even with her lying apparently at the point of death; I never could imagine a sense of fear coming near H. P. B. Finally came the anxious night when the doctors gave her up, and said that nothing could be done, it was impossible. She was then in a state of coma and had been so for some hours. The doctors said that she would pass **away** in that condition, and I knew, humanly speaking, that night's watch must be the last. I cannot here go into what happened, an experience I can never forget; but towards 8 a.m. H. P. B. suddenly opened her eyes and asked for her breakfast, the first time she had spoken naturally for two days. I went to meet the doctor, whose amazement at the change was very great. H. P. B. said, " Ah! doctor, you do not believe in our great Masters". From that time she steadily improved. The doctor insisted on her being sent to Europe as soon as possible; I was unable to go with her, my health having broken down with the strain, and I could not stand without crutches. Space fails me, and the rest must wait; but this I must say, in all the years I have known our Teacher and friend I have never known her utter one ungenerous word of her greatest enemy; she was the practical personification of charity and forgiveness, and was always ready to give another chance of doing better to any one who had failed her. It is said that "familiarity breeds contempt", but it is a striking fact that the more closely and intimately we were united to H. P. B. in everyday life, the more did we learn to respect, nay to reverence her. A wonderful and mysterious line of demarcation always

2

surrounded her, severing her inner spiritual life from her outer, and apparently ordinary one. Her every moment was devoted to the work she had been sent to do; nothing was too small or minute for her most careful attention. She passed away like a sentinel at his post, in the armchair in which she taught and wrote—the best and truest of Teachers, the most faithful and untiring of Messengers.

ISABEL COOPER-OAKLEY, F.T.S.

At Würzburg and Ostende.

IN the month of November, 1885, I went to Würzburg to visit Madame Blavatsky; I had met her previously in both France and England, but had had only a casual acquaintance with her. I found H. P. B. sick and weary of life, depressed both in mind and body, for she knew what a vast and important mission she had to fulfil, and how difficult it was to find those who were willing to give themselves up to the carrying out of the noble work which was her allotted task in life. She used often to deplore the indifference of the members of the T.S. in this respect, and she said that if she could only raise the veil for one moment, and let them see into the future, what a difference it would make; but each had to work out his own Karma and battle through his difficulties alone.

Madame Blavatsky was settled in comfortable apartments with lofty rooms and with the quiet surroundings she so much needed for the stupendous work in which she was engaged. Every morning at 6 a.m. she used to rise, having a good hour's work before her breakfast at 8 a.m., then, after having read her letters and newspapers she would again settle to her writing, sometimes calling me into the room to tell me that references from books and manuscripts had been given to her by her Master with the chapter and page quoted, and to ask me whether I could get friends to verify the correctness of these passages in different Public Libraries: for as she read everything reversed in the Astral Light, it would be easy for her to make mistakes in dates and numbers—and in some instances it was found that the number of the page had been reversed, for instance 23 would be found on page 32, etc.

Between one and two o'clock was Madame Blavatsky's dinner hour, the time varying to accommodate her work, and then without any repose she would immediately set herself at her table again, writing until six o'clock, when tea would be served. The old lady's relaxation during the evening would be her " Patiences ", laying out the cards while I read to her letters received during the day or scraps from newspapers which I thought might interest her. Between nine and ten o'clock H. P. B. retired to rest, usually taking some slight refreshment, and would read her Russian newspapers until midnight, when her lamp was put out, and all would be quiet until the next morning, when the usual routine recommenced. And so, day after day, the same unvarying life went on, only broken by the malicious Hodgson report which caused waves of disturbance to reach us from all sides. H. P. B. said to me one evening: "You cannot imagine what it is to feel so many adverse thoughts and currents directed against you; it is like the prickings of a thousand needles, and I have continually to be erecting a wall of protection around me". I asked her whether she knew from whom these unfriendly thoughts came, she answered: "Yes; unfortunately I do, and I am always trying to shut my eyes so as not to see and know"; and to prove to me that this was the case, she would tell me of letters that had been written, quoting passages from them, and these actually arrived a day or two afterwards, I being able to verify the correctness of the sentences.

All who have known and loved H. P. B. have felt what a charm there was about her, how truly kind and loveable she was; at times such a bright childish nature seemed to beam around her, and a spirit of joyous fun would sparkle in her whole countenance, and cause the most winning expression that I have ever seen on a human face. One of the marvels of her character was, that to everybody she was different. I have never seen her treat two persons alike. The weak traits in every one's character were known to her at once, and the extraordinary way in which she would probe them was surprising. By those who lived in daily contact with her the knowledge of *Self* was gradually acquired, and by those who chose to benefit by her practical way of teaching progress could be made. But to many of her pupils the process was unpalatable, for it is never pleasant to be brought face to face with one's own weaknesses; and so many turned from her, but those who could stand the test, and remain true to her, would recognise within themselves the inner development which alone leads to Occultism. A truer and more faithful friend one could never have than H. P. B., and I think it the greatest blessing of my life to have lived with her in such close intimacy, and until my death I shall try and further the noble cause for which she slaved and suffered so much.

I shall not speak of phenomena in this paper, for my personal testimony can be of no use to anybody but myself, except to satisfy curiosity; all I can say is, that phenomena occurred daily both in Würzburg and in Ostende, where I spent a second winter with Madame Blavatsky. In fact what people call phenomena seemed to me the ordinary natural occurrences of daily life, so used did I become to them; and true it is, that we only call phenomena that which we are unable fully to explain—and the shooting stars, the growth of trees, in fact all nature around us is one vast phenomenon which if witnessed but rarely would fill us with far more incredulity and astonishment than the ringing of astral bells, etc.

Our stay in Würzburg was only interrupted by casual visitors, the last being Madame Gebhard and Miss Kislingbury in the month of May, 1886. I parted with H. P. B. at the station, leaving her with Miss Kislingbury, who was to accompany her to Ostende, while I went with Madame Gebhard to Kempten, where we were met by Dr. Franz Hartmann, who showed us that strange, weird and mystical town.

In October, 1886, I joined H. P. B. in Ostende, and found her settled in comfortable enough quarters; she welcomed me with all the warmth of her genial nature, and was, I think, as truly glad to have me as I was to be with her. We recommenced our monotonous but interesting life, the thread being taken up from where it was last broken, and I watched with delight how the piles of manuscript for the *S.D.* were increasing. Our near vicinity to England caused people once more to come buzzing round H. P. B., and we received several visitors, amongst whom were Mrs. Kingsford and Mr. Maitland, and it was a pleasure to listen to the conversation of three such highly gifted intellects on all the points of resemblance between Western and Eastern Occultism, but still with my further and later experience of H. P. B. and her teachings it is marvellous to me how she kept safely locked within her own breast the occult knowledge which she has lately been permitted to give to a few of her pupils.

Towards the end of the winter H. P. B. became very ill; her kidneys were affected, and after some days of intense suffering the Belgian doctor told me that he despaired of her life. I telegraphed to Madame Gebhard, who had been a true and sincere friend of hers for many years, and also to Mr. Ashton Ellis, a member of the T.S. and a clever doctor, both responded to my call and helped me through those trying and anxious days, and in the end Mr. Ellis' wise treatment pulled her through the dangerous crisis. As H. P. B. was slowly recovering other friends came. Dr. Keightley and also Mr. Bertram Keightley were among these, and they both persuaded Madame Blavatsky to go and spend the summer in England in a small cottage which was taken for her at Norwood.

I then left Ostende, Madame Gebhard kindly remaining with the old lady until she felt equal to undertaking the journey to London. During the same summer, while I was at home in Sweden, H. P. B. wrote to me that there was a proposal to take a house in London with the Keightleys, to form a centre for theosophical work in England; she wrote: "Now at last I begin to see my way clearly before me, and Master's work can be done if you will only agree to come and live with us. I have told the Keightleys that without you their project must fall to the ground," etc., etc. I replied that I would take a share in the house, and hoped that a nucleus of earnest members would be formed to carry on the work and her mission in life.

I came to England in August, 1887, found H. P. B. at Norwood, and shortly afterwards we moved into 17, Lansdowne Road, Holland Park, and then began a new, difficult and often painful life. Trials followed each other in quick succession, but the very outcome of all these trials and worries was the development of the Society and the spreading of theosophical truths.

Madame Blavatsky was at home every Saturday afternoon, and visitors came every evening, crowds of people ; some out of curiosity, others with a true desire to learn about Theosophy, and a few attracted by her personality. To watch the varied way in which H. P. B. would receive each new arrival was in itself a study, and later events have proved that her knowledge of character was unique. At times she would seem to grow and expand in intellect and the force and power with which she would put forward her vast knowledge would seize those present with awe ; at other times she only talked of the most trivial things, and her hearers would go away quite satisfied with themselves, feeling that they were vastly her superiors. But I have only a certain space allotted to me and must close these few lines.

The house in Lansdowne Road became too small for the requirements of the workers who had gathered around us, and so in July, 1890, we moved into 19, Avenue Road, which became the Headquarters of the European T.S.

Others having gradually shared with me in the daily care and attention with which it had hitherto been my privilege and pleasure to surround H. P. B., I must leave it to their eloquence to give you a description of her life, and slowly declining health ; and now our beloved friend and teacher has gone, but H. P. B.'s work still remains to be finished, and it is only by the way in which we carry on that work that we can prove to the world how intense has been our love and gratitude to the noblest and grandest woman this century will have produced.

CONSTANCE WACHTMEISTER, F.T.S.

A Word from Mr. Sinnett.

I HAVE been writing about Madame Blavatsky at considerable length for another periodical and have thus endeavoured to convey to the exoteric public some idea of the grandeur of the work she has been carrying on in the life just closed. Invited to contribute some remarks concerning my long friendship with her to the magazine she herself founded, I prefer now to avoid any direct repetition of external impressions concerning her wonderful attributes and faculties, and to deal instead with hints I have received from herself, and in other ways, from time to time, as to the probable course of her own evolution in the future. For many years past she has spoken to me at intervals of the hopes she entertained in reference to the destinies in store for her when permitted to lay down the burden of the incarnation now exhausted. All theosophists who have profited by the illumination she was able to shed upon the principles governing individual human progress, will realise two conclusions about her as practically certain. The life just over cannot have been that in which she first began her occult career, and it will certainly not be followed by a normal return in her case to an ordinary period of devachanic rest. She must have been considerably advanced in preparatory initiation before she became H. P. B., and the hard and faithful work she has now been performing for so many years in the service of those who are never ungrateful, will mean inevitably that kind of reward which will best subserve her further spiritual progress. I do not know how far she may have elucidated the matter to others, but I see no reason for reticence in regard to her more recent incarnations; in reference to which, indeed, she never gave me any details, and led me to believe that she was unacquainted with details. But as to the broad fact I have no personal doubt. Her very last incarnation before this one just completed was in the person of a member of her own recent family, an aunt who died prematurely; and that existence does not seem to have served her advancement in any important degree. Before that she had been a Hindoo woman of considerable occult attainments, with eager hopes and aspirations concerning the people to whom she then belonged. Her transfer to another nationality seems to have been connected in some way with a belief on her part that she would be better able from the fulcrum of a European birth to further the interest of the Hindoo race.

As regards the future—or may we say as regards the present?—it seems very unlikely that she would have another female incarnation in succession to her last. The highest teaching has been to the effect that alternations occur in almost all cases after a short series of incarnations in the same sex. Her own wish in this matter pointed very strongly to a masculine incarnation this time, and her expectation that this wish would be realised was very confident.

Many readers of LUCIFER will be aware that the abnormal incarnations of those whose Karma has lifted them above the operation of automatic laws are of two kinds. The Chela-Ego may be linked with a newly forming organism, and be born as a child in the ordinary way—though destined in such a case to recover recollection of the previous life as soon as the new body should attain maturity; or it may be transferred with violence, so to speak, to an already mature body, adapted to serve as a vehicle for its further manifestations and progress, if such a body happens to be ready at the right moment; that is to say if its former tenant happens to be provided for in some other way. To meet such an opportunity as this it would be necessary that the right moment should be seized for effecting the transfer, and it might be expected therefore that any one in whose interest such a transfer was to be accomplished, would be called at a moment's notice, would in conventional language, die very suddenly. Now it is a striking fact about Madame Blavatsky's "death" that ill as she often has been of late, and impossible though it might have been to have kept her organism in activity much longer, she was physically better on the day she died than she had been for several days previously, and was congratulated that morning by her doctor on having got over the attack she had been troubled with. Her death just when it occurred was an absolutely unexpected event, and could probably not be assigned to any specific physical cause. On two or three occasions during the last half dozen years she has been definitely given over by her doctors and declared incapable of living another day. In such crises she has been rescued at the last moment, evidently by the exercise of occult power; whereas on the present occasion, when there was no apparent need for her to die at all, she closes her eyes and passes away in an instant.

To me the inference seems very plain and points among other conclusions to the *possibility* that the new personality she may now have been clothed with, if already mature, may in the progress of events be identified by some of us now living before we in turn are called upon—or permitted—to use whichever phrase best suits our internal condition of mind—to pass through the great change ourselves.

A. P. SINNETT, F.T.S.

A Memory of Madame Blavatsky.

THE first and earliest impression I received from Madame Blavatsky was the feeling of the power and largeness of her individuality; as though I were in the presence of one of the primal forces of Nature.

I remember that the talk turned upon the great leaders of materialism, —then filling a larger space in the public eye than now—and their dogmatic negative of the soul and of spiritual forces. Madame Blavatsky's attitude in the discussion was not combative, hardly even argumentative; still she left in the mind the conviction of the utter futility of material reasoning, and this not by any subtle logic or controversial skill, but as though a living and immortal spirit by its mere presence at once confuted the negation of spiritual life.

This sense of the power of individuality was not what one has felt in the presence of some great personality, who dominates and dwarfs surrounding persons into insignificance, and tyrannously overrides their independence. It was rather the sense of a profound deep-seated reality, an exhaustless power of resistance, a spirit built on the very depths of Nature, and reaching down to the primæval eternities of Truth.

Gradually apparent under this dominant impression of power, arose a subtle sense of great gentleness and kindliness, an unfailing readiness to forget herself entirely and to throw herself heartily into the life of others.

Another side of Madame Blavatsky's character unfolded itself more slowly—the great light and piercing insight of her soul.

One was lulled, as it were, by the sympathetic personality, and tranquillised by the feeling of balanced power, so that at first this quality of inner light might remain unnoted, till some sudden turn of thought or change of feeling opened the eyes, and one recognized the presence of a denizen of eternity.

Everyone has noticed, in travelling through some wild and mountainous country, that the vast masses and depths of the hills and valleys are often hid and remain unapparent ; the mind and eye are held by the gentler graces of nature, the trees, the birds, and the flowers ; and some ridge is ascended imperceptibly, till suddenly the crest is reached, and the mind is startled by the vast perspective swiftly unfolded before it.

These startling, unexpected glimpses into profundity, I have often felt in Madame Blavatsky's presence, when the richness and sympathy of her character had almost tempted one to believe her a fascinating personality, and nothing more.

All through her life, the dominant note of Madame Blavatsky's character has been power ; in early years, power without light ; then later, power and light in equal balance. The earliest record of her life shews her as a strong and dominant personality, always deeply impressing herself on her surroundings, and overriding and dominating the personalities of others, imperiously, often tyrannically, yet with an ever-present imperious generosity and gentleness ; a deep generosity of thought, an almost incredible generosity of action ; a powerful personality, using its power often extravagantly, often unwisely, often unjustly.

Then the light dawned for her, and the chaotic strength of her nature was illuminated, harmonised, purified, and with the same dominant power she prepared to deliver her message to mankind, the message of the strong to the weak, of one who stood within the circle of light to those in the darkness without.

With unparalleled force, she asserted the soul ; with transcendent strength she taught the reality of spirit, by living the life, and manifesting the energies of an immortal.

She cast herself with torrential force against the dark noxious clouds of evil and ignorance that envelope and poison human life ; the rift in their leaden masses through which, high above, we catch a glimpse of the blue, bears testimony to the greatness of the power that rent them asunder.

She was a personality of such magnitude as to divide the world into her adherents and her opponents, leaving none indifferent between ; the test of the force of her nature is as much the fierce animosity of her enemies as the loving devotion of her friends. Such was the power and dominance of her individuality, that, in comparison with hers, all other souls seemed inert.

An immortal spirit, she had the courage to live as an immortal spirit, and to subject material nature and the base forces of life to the powers of her immortality; she perpetually took her stand on the realities of spiritual nature, and consistently refused to admit the dominant tyranny of the material world.

And this dominant power and this clear interior light were united to a nature of wonderful kindness, wonderful gentleness, and absolute self-forgetfulness and forgiveness of wrong.

Nothing in her was more remarkable, nothing more truly stamped her as one of the elect, than the great humility of her character, ready to deny and ignore all its own splendid endowments, in order to bring into light the qualities of others. This humility was no mere affectation, no mere trick to call up admiration and wonder, but the profoundly sincere expression of her own nature; an expression as deep and real as Sir Isaac Newton's comparison of himself, after a life of unequalled achievement, to a little child gathering shells by the shore of the ocean.

Madame Blavatsky's nature was like a mountain torrent, having its source in some deep, clear lake above the clouds, and impetuously carrying down to the valleys the riches of the mountains, to spread them over the hungry and thirsty plains below; to give them new life and fertility, and the promise of a richer harvest in due season; and amongst the commoner gifts of the mountains, bringing now and then grains of gold and precious gems, and scattering them like Pactolus, over the sands of the valley; and ever and anon the dwellers of the valley, finding these rarer treasures, see in them the promise of the deeper wealth of the mountains, and vow to themselves never to give up the search for the great treasure until they die.

Such was Madame Blavatsky in her life; and now that she is dead, her death seems to have taken away from us half the savour of life; and her absence to have withdrawn one of the great incentives to living.

But to hallow the loneliness of her death, she has left us the great lesson of her life, a life true to itself, true to its Spirit, true to its God.

One who stood beside her, so calm and quiescent in death, could never believe that that torrential nature, that splendid power, had ceased to be; with the feeling of loss at her departure came the conviction far stronger than reason or logic that a power like hers could not be quenched by death, that a great soul like hers could never cease to be.

And so has gone from amongst us a soul of singular power, of singular light, of singular sweetness. Her life has given a new nobility to life; and Death has become more kindly by her death.

CHARLES JOHNSTON, F.T.S.

"Yours till Death and after, H.P.B."

SUCH has been the manner in which our beloved teacher and friend always concluded her letters to me. And now, though we are all of us committing to paper some account of that departed friend and teacher, I feel ever near and ever potent the magic of that resistless power, as of a mighty rushing river, which those who wholly trusted her always came to understand. Fortunate indeed is that Karma which, for all the years since I first met her, in 1875, has kept me faithful to the friend who, masquerading under the outer *mortal* garment known as H. P. Blavatsky, was ever faithful to me, ever kind, ever the teacher and the guide.

In 1874, in the City of New York, I first met H. P. B. in this life. By her request, sent through Colonel H. S. Olcott, the call was made in her rooms in Irving Place, when then, as afterwards, through the remainder of her stormy career, she was surrounded by the anxious, the intellectual, the bohemian, the rich and the poor. It was her eye that attracted me, the eye of one whom I must have known in lives long passed away. She looked at me in recognition at that first hour, and never since has that look changed. Not as a questioner of philosophies did I come before her, not as one groping in the dark for lights that schools and fanciful theories had obscured, but as one who, wandering many periods through the corridors of life, was seeking the friends who could show where the designs for the work had been hidden. And true to the call she responded, revealing the plans once again, and speaking no words to explain, simply pointed them out and went on with the task. It was as if but the evening before we had parted, leaving yet to be done some detail of a task taken up with one common end ; it was teacher and pupil, elder brother and younger, both bent on the one single end, but she with the power and the knowledge that belong but to lions and sages. So, friends from the first, I felt safe. Others I know have looked with suspicion on an appearance they could not fathom, and though it is true they adduce many proofs which, hugged to the breast, would damn sages and gods, yet it is only through blindness they failed to see the lion's glance, the diamond heart of H. P. B.

The entire space of this whole magazine would not suffice to enable me to record the phenomena she performed for me through all these years, nor would I wish to put them down. As she so often said, they prove nothing but only lead some souls to doubt and others to despair. And again, I do not think they were done just for me, but only that in those early days she was laying down the lines of force all over the land and I, so fortunate, was at the centre of the energy and saw the play of forces in visible phenomena. The explanation has been offered by some too anxious friends that the earlier phenomena were mistakes in judgment, attempted to be rectified in later years by confining their area and limiting their number, but until some one shall produce in the writing of H. P. B. her concurrence with that view, I shall hold to her own explanation made in advance and never changed. That I have given above. For many it is easier to take refuge behind a charge of bad judgment than to understand the strange and powerful laws which control in matters such as these.

Amid all the turmoil of her life, above the din produced by those who charged her with deceit and fraud and others who defended, while month after month, and year after year, witnessed men and women entering the theosophical movement only to leave it soon with malignant phrases for H. P. B., there stands a fact we all might imitate—devotion absolute to her Master. " It was He", she writes, " who told me to devote myself to this, and I will never disobey and never turn back."

In 1888 she wrote to me privately :—

" Well, my *only* friend, you ought to know better. Look into my life and try to realize it—in its outer course at least, as the rest is hidden. I am under the curse of ever writing, as the wandering Jew was under that of being ever on the move, never stopping one moment to rest. Three ordinary healthy persons could hardly do what *I have* to do. I live an artificial life ; I am an automaton running full steam until the power of generating steam stops, and then—good-bye ! ✧ ✧ ✧ Night before last I was shown a bird's-eye view of the Theosophical Societies. I saw a few earnest reliable Theosophists in a death struggle with the world in general, with other—nominal but ambitious—Theosophists. The former are greater in numbers than you may think, and *they prevailed*, as you in *America will prevail*, if you only remain staunch to the Master's programme and true to yourselves. And last night I saw ✧✧✧ and now I feel strong—such as I am in my body—and ready to fight for Theosophy and the few *true* ones to my last breath. The defending forces have to be judiciously—so scanty they are—distributed over the globe, wherever Theosophy is struggling against the powers of darkness."

Such she ever was ; devoted to Theosophy and the Society organized to carry out a programme embracing the world in its scope. Willing in the service of the cause to offer up hope, money, reputation, life itself, provided the Society might be saved from every hurt, whether small or great. And thus bound body, heart and soul to this entity called the Theosophical Society, bound to protect it at all hazards, in face of every loss, she often incurred the resentment of many who became her friends but would not always care for the infant organization as she had sworn to do. And when they acted as if opposed to the Society, her instant opposition seemed to them to nullify professions of friendship. Thus she had but few friends, for it required a keen insight, untinged with personal feeling, to see even a small part of the real H. P. Blavatsky.

But was her object merely to form a Society whose strength should lie in numbers ? Not so. She worked under directors who, operating from *behind the scene*, knew that the Theosophical Society was, and was to be, the nucleus from which help might spread to all the people of the day, without thanks and without acknowledgment. Once, in London, I asked her what was the chance of drawing the people into the Society in view of the enormous disproportion between the number of members and the millions of Europe and America who neither knew of nor cared for it. Leaning back in her chair, in which she was sitting before her writing desk, she said :—

" When you consider and remember those days in 1875 and after, in which you could not find any people interested in your thoughts, and now look at the wide-spreading influence of theosophical ideas—however labelled —it is not so bad. We are not working merely that people may call themselves *Theosophists*, but that the doctrines we cherish may affect and leaven the whole mind of this century. This alone can be accomplished by a small earnest band of workers, who work for no human reward, no earthly recognition, but who, supported and sustained by a belief in that Universal Brotherhood of which our Masters are a part, work steadily, faithfully, in understanding and putting forth for consideration the doctrines of life and duty that have come down to us from immemorial time. Falter not so long as a few devoted ones will work to keep the nucleus existing. You were not directed to found and realise a Universal Brotherhood, but to form the nucleus for one ; for it is only when the nucleus is formed that the accumulations can begin that will end in future years, however far, in the formation of that body which we have in view."

H. P. B. had a lion heart, and on the work traced out for her she had the lion's grasp ; let us, her friends, companions and disciples, sustain ourselves in carrying out the designs laid down on the trestle-board, by the memory of her devotion and the consciousness that behind her task there stood, and still remain, those Elder Brothers who, above the clatter and the din of our battle, ever see the end and direct the forces distributed in array for the salvation of " that great orphan—Humanity".

WILLIAM Q. JUDGE, F.T.S.

As I knew her.

" Endurance is the crowning quality,
And patience all the passion of great hearts."

Lowell.

ENDURANCE and patience have certainly been the crowning qualities of H. P. B. as I have known her during the last years of her life, and as I have heard of her from those fortunate enough to have known her for more years than I can count during her present life. The most salient of her characteristics was implied in these crowning qualities ; it was that of strength, steady strength, unyielding as a rock. I have seen weaklings dash themselves up against her, and then whimper that she was hard ; but

I have also seen her face to face with a woman who had been her cruel enemy—but who was in distress and, as I uncharitably thought, *therefore* repentant—and every feature was radiant with a divine compassion, which only did not forgive because it would not admit that it had been outraged. The hardness which can be tender is the hardness which is needed in our mollient Western life, in which one is sick of the shams that pass for value, of the falseness that stabs with a smile, and betrays with a kiss. Unconventional, H. P. B. was always called, and the adjective was appropriate. She did not regard society conventions as natural laws, and she preferred frankness to compliment. Above all she had the sense of proportion, and that "rarest sense of all, common sense". She did not think that all natural piety was trampled under foot when a woman smoked cigarettes, nor that every bond which held society together was ruptured when some solecism in manners was committed. A traveller in many lands, she had seen social customs so various that one or another was to her as unimportant as wearing a hat, a turban, or a fez, and she laughed at all the crude insular British ideas that a man's merit depended on his agreement with our own notions. On the other hand, she was rigidity itself in the weightier matters of the law; and had it not been for the injury the writers were doing themselves by the foulnesses they flung at her, I could often have almost laughed at the very absurdity of the contrast between the fraudulent charlatan and profligate they pictured, and the H. P. B. I lived beside, with honour as sensitive as that of the "very gentil parfait knyghte", truth flawless as a diamond, purity which had in it much of a child's candour mingled with the sternness which could hold it scatheless against attack. Apart from all questions of moral obligation, H. P. B. was far too proud a woman, in her personality, to tell a lie. Brought up amid the highest born of the Russian nobility, inheriting much of their haughty contempt for the people around them, she would not have condescended to justify herself by untruth; she did not sufficiently care for "what people would say" to stoop to any subterfuge to defend herself. Indeed some of the earlier slanders took their rise in this very recklessness of public opinion. And when to this was added the occult training that hardens the chela against all outside judgments, and placing him ever at the tribunal of his Higher Self renders him indifferent to all lesser condemnation, it will readily be seen that the motives to untruthfulness which move ordinary people were absent. And this is apart from the deeper facts of the case, of which it would be idle here to speak, and of which it must suffice to say that no high Occultist can dare to lie for personal gain or personal defence.

It used to be said that the devil paid his servants well in this life, in whatever fashion he might recover the debt in another; but verily if, as the pious say, she was one of his emissaries, the gold mines of Sheol must be giving out. For in these later days H. P. B. was a very poor woman, and I have known her hard pressed for a sovereign many a time. Then some devoted admirer would send her money, and away it went, to the Theosophical Society, to a distressed friend, to an old servant in want, to some family whose starvation I might have mentioned. It was a royally generous nature, that of H. P. B., always needing some channel into which it might flow over ; money, clothes, jewels, anything she had, she flung it away with both hands to the first who was in want.

Looking at her generally, she was much more of a man than a woman. Outspoken, decided, prompt, strong-willed, genial, humorous, free from pettiness and without malignity, she was wholly different from the average female type. She judged always on large lines, with wide tolerance for diversities of character and of thought, indifferent to outward appearances if the inner man were just and true.

Personally, one of the greatest services she rendered me was placing at my service as an aid to self-knowledge her own deep insight into character. I have laughed to myself when I have heard folk say that " Madame Blavatsky must be a very bad judge of character, or she would never have trusted people who afterwards betrayed her ". They did not know that her rule was to give every one his chance, and she never recked if in thus doing she ran risk of injury to herself. It was always herself she gave away to such persons—never the Society, nor any knowledge they could use to the injury of others. I watched the course of one such case, a young Judas who pretended friendship, who was admitted by her to stay in her house, who tried ineffectively to find out " secrets ", and went away finally to attack her and try to betray. She talked to him freely enough, hindered him in none of his enquiries, tried to lead him the right way, but once or twice I caught those strange eyes of hers, of which so much has been said, looking him through with a deep pathetic gaze, turning away at last with a half-breathed sigh. But when anyone was really seeking that most difficult of all knowledge, self-knowledge, then she would use her rare power of insight, would warn of hidden dangers, point to concealed characteristics, unravel the tangled threads of half-understood or non-understood qualities and defects, and thus guide the student in his efforts to know himself, and to escape from the web of illusion. Over and over again, in my own case, she has led me straight to hidden motive, to concealed weakness, to covered pitfall, and any of her pupils who could bear her scrutiny and criticism without resentment might be sure of similar aid.

As teacher H. P. B. was inspiring and suggestive, not didactic. She could only teach effectively when the student was thoroughly in touch with her, and could fill with quick intuition the gaps she left in her outline. In such cases she would throw out thought after thought, with wonderful wealth of illustrations from the most widely separated sources, the thoughts often unrelated on the surface, but always found, on careful re-study afterwards, to be links thrown, as it were, into light of some unbroken chain. The intervening links had been left in shadow, and if the student could throw them also into light, by the use of his own intuition, it was well. But where the student's mind gave no response to hers, where her quick blows startled no spark to leap forth in answer from the rock, to such H. P. B. remained always enigmatic, obscure, involved, lost in maze of metaphysics, and she proved as unsatisfactory to them as they were hopeless to her.

Of late, H. P. B. led a very secluded life; she would close her doors for days, sometimes for weeks, against those who were nearest to her, and we understand now how she was preparing all for the approaching change. And to us who lived with her the change is less than many, perhaps, may suppose. Our nearness to her was not that of the bodily presence, it was that far closer tie which ever binds together teacher and pupil in the venerable philosophy which it was her mission to impart. To us, the mere fact that she has flung off the worn-out garment of her personality in no wise alters the relation between her and us; those of us who were with her in past lives have been separated physically before through " the change that men call death ", and have found each other again on return to " life " on earth. What has been shall be, and in the true life no separation is possible. For many a year past, her life has been one long torture; she stood at the centre of a whirl of forces spiritual and psychic, exposed at the same time to the pressure of the material plane. Alone, with none who could wholly understand her, misunderstood, wronged, insulted, and even when loved mostly loved in a mistaken way, none except her peers can tell what a hell upon earth her life has been. That she is out of it, is matter for rejoicing, not for sorrowing for those who really loved *her*, not themselves in her. The work to which she gave her life is now ours to carry on; the forces behind it are not weakened because H. P. Blavatsky has departed. It is the work of the Brotherhood, not of any one individual, and while the Brotherhood lives and works neither doubt nor despair can touch their disciples. We have but to do our duty: success, as the world counts it, is a thing of no account.

ANNIE BESANT, F.T.S.

The Last Two Years.

I HAD previously stayed at 17, Lansdowne Road, during my vacations. but it was not until the beginning of August, 1889, that I came to work permanently with H. P. B. She was away in Jersey then, and the copy and proofs of LUCIFER were being busily transmitted backwards and forwards to the accompaniment of an infinity of characteristic notes and telegrams. I had only time to review two books before a pressing telegram came from H. P. B., and I started for Jersey. What a warm greeting there was in the porch of that honeysuckle-covered house, and what a fuss to have everything comfortable for the new comer !

It has often been a surprise to me that the chief of the accusations and slanders brought against H. P. B. have been those of fraud and concealment, and I can only account for it by the fact that those who make such accusations (save the Coulomb woman), have never known her. According to my experience, she was ever over-trustful of others and quite prodigal in her frankness. As an instance, no sooner had I arrived than she gave me the run of all her papers, and set me to work on a pile of correspondence that would otherwise have remained unanswered till doomsday; for if she detested anything, it was answering letters. I then was initiated into the mysteries of LUCIFER, and soon had my hands full with transmission of directions, alterations, and counter-directions to Bertram Keightley, who was then Sub-editor, for in those days H. P. B. *would* not let one word go into LUCIFER until she had seen and reseen it, and she added to and cut up the proofs until the last moment.

One day, shortly after my arrival, H. P. B. came into my room unexpectedly with a manuscript and handed it to me, saying, " Read that, old man, and tell me what you think of it ". It was the MS. of the third part of the *Voice of the Silence*, and while I read she sat and smoked her cigarettes, tapping her foot on the floor, as was often her habit. I read on, forgetting her presence in the beauty and sublimity of the theme until she broke in upon my silence with, " Well ? " I told her it was the grandest thing in all our theosophical literature, and tried, contrary to my habit, to convey in words some of the enthusiasm that I felt. But even then H. P. B. was not content with her work, and expressed the greatest apprehension that she had failed to do justice to the original in her translation, and could hardly be persuaded that she had done well. This was one of her chief characteristics. Never was she confident of her own literary work, and cheerfully listened to all criticisms, even from persons who should have remained silent. Strangely enough she was always most timorous of her best articles and works and most confident of her polemical writings.

When we returned to Lansdowne Road, one of those changes, so familiar to those who have worked with H. P. B., occurred, and both Dr. Archibald Keightley and Bertram Keightley left for abroad, the former on a voyage round the world, the latter to lecture in the United States. And so their duties came mostly to me, and I gradually began to see a great deal of her alone at her work owing to the necessity of the case.

Let me see if I can give some idea of how the work was done.

To begin with there was LUCIFER, of which she was then sole editor. In the first place H. P. B. never read an MS., she required to see it in proof and then mostly " averaged " its contents. What she *was* particular about was the length of the copy, and she used to laboriously count the number of words in each paper, and would never be persuaded of the accuracy of my count when I in my turn " averaged " the length. If I suggested that mine was the most expeditious method, she would proceed to tell me some home truths about Oxford and Cambridge education, and I often thought she used to continue her primitive methods of arithmetical computation on purpose to cure me of my impatience and my confidence in my own superiority. Another great thing was the arranging of the different articles. In those days she would never entrust this to any other hand, and the measuring of everything was a painful operation.

Getting LUCIFER through the press was invariably a rush, for she generally wrote her leader the last thing and, having been used to it, considered the printers, if anybody, were to blame if it did not appear in time. But all that was soon changed when Annie Besant became co-editor and H. P. B. found that it was not necessary to do everything herself.

Then there was the correspondence, voluminous enough in all conscience, from all parts of the world and from "all sorts and conditions of men" and women truly. H. P. B. was very laconic, sometimes even epigrammatic, in her directions as to answering it, and gradually became even more silent, so that I had often to risk her displeasure in pressing for a reply or in trying to persuade her to answer some letter of great importance herself. It was comparatively easy to get the morning mail in safe keeping, but letters arriving by later posts were a difficulty; for H. P. B. sternly refused all access to her room and, to make up for this, used to carefully put away the important letters in hiding places so as to give them to me later, while she left the rest to their fate. The plan was not a good one; for she mostly forgot her hiding-place and I often could not rescue the rest of the waifs and strays from among her MS. at all, for she would let no one touch the work she was actually engaged upon, and so they had to go, to be answered when finally unearthed at some distant date. But gradually too we found out better methods, and latterly I have not had to play so many games of hide and seek.

The first hour in the morning after breakfast during those two years will ever remain with me a pleasant recollection. Everything was so unconventional. I used to sit on the arm of her great armchair and obediently smoke the cigarette she offered, while she opened the letters, told me what she wanted done and signed diplomas and certificates, the latter under great pressure, however, for she detested such mechanical work. It was exciting and instructive too, for in our large Society there were always crises of more or less gravity. The many disputes came to her for settlement, and the many attacks had to be met and counteracted by her. So it was that I learnt much of human character and of the inner working of the Society and how the life of it depended upon her. Many an evidence too had I of her prodigal generosity, and many a gift did I transmit to a poor Theosophist or employ for theosophical purposes under strict promise of secrecy, although she thereby frequently came to the bottom of her "stocking".

Though H. P. B. left much of her correspondence to me, still it was not without a distinct supervision, for she would suddenly call for a reply that had not yet gone out or for the copy of an old letter, without any warning, and if there were any mistakes, the lecture I received was not reassuring to my discomfiture. One thing she was always impressing upon me, and this was to develope a sense of the " fitness of things", and she was merciless if this law of harmony were broken, leaving no loop-hole of escape, and listening to no excuse, with her over-powering reason and knowledge, which in spite of its apparently disconnected expression, always went home ; although, indeed, the minute afterward, she was again the affectionate friend and elder brother, shall I even say, comrade, as she alone knew how to be.

One of the greatest proofs to me of H. P. B.'s extraordinary gifts and ability, if proof were needed in the face of the manifest sincerity of her life-work, was the way in which she wrote her articles and books. I knew every book she had in her small library, and yet day after day she would produce quantities of MS. abounding in quotations, which were seldom inaccurate. I remember almost the last day she sat at her desk, going into her room to query two Greek words in a quotation, and telling her they were inaccurate. Now though H. P. B. could in her early years speak modern Greek and had been taught ancient Greek by her grandmother, she had long forgotten it for all purposes of accuracy, and the correction of the words I objected to required precise scholarship. " Where did you get it from, H. P. B. ? " I asked. " I'm sure I don't know, my dear ", was her somewhat discouraging rejoinder. " I saw it ! " adding that she was certain that she was right, for now she remembered when she wrote the particular passage referred to. However, I persuaded her that there was some mistake, and finally she said, " Well, of course you are a great Greek pundit, I know, but you're not going to sit upon me always. I'll try if I can see it again, and now get out ", meaning that she wanted to go on with her work, or at any rate had had enough of me. About two minutes after-wards, she called me in again and presented me with a scrap of paper on which she had written the two words quite correctly, saying, " Well, I sup-pose you'll be a greater pundit than ever after this ! "

The above is one instance out of many, but it will little profit to narrate them, for they mean nothing to anyone but the eye-witness, and the public is quite content with its own infallibility of judgment and prefers to remain myopic.

In the evenings, H. P. B. liked to have the household round her, and tried her best to force us to abandon work for a couple of hours. She herself played her eternal game of solitaire, which she very occasionally varied with a game of dummy whist. Many have questioned why H. P. B. always "made her cards" in the evening, and those of us who have learned by experience that H. P. B. did nothing without a reason, deduced logically that there was also reason in the cards. The evening was the time for anecdotes, for hints on occultism, for an infinity of useful information. There was, however, no order about it, and no one could count on hearing this or that, or getting an answer to a question. We had to wait for the opportunity, and never regretted the waiting when the opportunity came.

When we moved to our present Headquarters, many things were changed. Looking back it now seems almost as if H. P. B. had got things in training for leaving us at any moment, though apparently preparations were being made in which she herself and her continued residence with us were the principal factors.

Ever since she went to Brighton in the early part of last year she has suffered most cruelly in her physical body, and been unable to work as she used to. But we always lived in great expectations of restitution to at any rate her normal state of health. At Lansdowne Road she used always to be pleased to receive visitors, and nearly every evening they came in to see her. But in Avenue Road she gradually began to isolate herself more and more, so that often she would not receive even the members of the household in the evening unless she especially sent for them. Then again, she was strangely quiet latterly, rarely showing the great energy that was her peculiar characteristic. Still the same indomitable will was there, though her body was worn out, for she worked on at her desk even when she ought to have been in bed, or in her coffin. The very night before she left us, she insisted on going into her working room and playing her cards. It was indeed a last and supreme effort of will, for she was so weak that she could hardly speak or hold up her head. And thus the influenza claimed its greatest victim. Such at least is the opinion of one who regards it as his chiefest honour to have been the last of H.P.B.'s Private Secretaries.

G. R. S. MEAD, F.T.S.

What she is to me.

TWO years ago Annie Besant and I saw H. P. B. for the first time, and now it is not many days since I stood by her lily-covered coffin and took my last lingering look at the personality of the marvellous woman who had revolutionised the lives of my colleague and myself. Two years are but little as men count time, but these two have been so pregnant with soul-life that the old days before them seem ages away. If it be true that life should be counted by epochs of the mind, then life, from the day that I first clasped H. P. B.'s hand to the moment when, majestic in her death sleep, I helped to wreathe around her body the palms from that far-off East which she loved so well, was richer, fuller, longer to me than a generation of the outward turmoil which has its little day and then is gone. I went to her a materialist, she left me a Theosophist, and between these two there is a great gulf fixed. Over that gulf she bridged the way. She was my spiritual mother, and never had child a more loving, a more patient, a more tender guide.

It was in the old Lansdowne Road days. Beset with problems of life and mind that our materialism could not solve, dwelling intellectually on what are now to us the inhospitable shores of agnosticism, Annie Besant and I ever craved more light. We had read the *Occult World*, and in bye-gone years we had heard—who had not?—of the strange woman whose life seemed to be a contradiction of our most cherished theories, but as yet the philosophy of the book was to us but assertion, the life of the woman a career which we had no means of examining. Sceptical, critical, trained by long years of public controversy to demand the most rigid scientific proof of things which were outside our experience, Theosophy was to us an unknown, and, as it then seemed, an impossible land. And yet it fascinated, for it promised much, and with talking, with reading, the fascination grew. With the fascination also grew the desire to know, and so, on an ever-to-be remembered evening, with a letter of introduction from Mr. W. T. Stead, then editor of the *Pall Mall Gazette*, as our passport, we found ourselves face to face, in the drawing room of 17, Lansdowne Road, with the woman whom we afterwards learned to know and to love as the most wonderful woman of her time.

I was not foolish enough to look for miracles, I did not expect to see Madame Blavatsky float, nor did I crave for materialised teacups, but I did want to hear about Theosophy, and I did not hear much. She whom we were there to see was a stout, unwieldy lady, playing Russian " Patience ", and keeping up a stream of conversation on nearly every subject except the one which was just then nearest our minds. No attempt at proselyting, no attempt to " fix " us, (we were *not* hypnotised!) but all the while the wonderful eyes were flashing light, and, in spite of the bodily infirmity which was even then painfully apparent, there was a reserve of power which gave the impression that we were seeing, not the real woman, but only the surface character of some one who had endured much, and who knew much.

I tried to keep an open impartial mind, and I believe I succeeded. I was genuinely anxious to learn, but I was critical and on the watch for the slightest attempt at hoodwinking. When I afterwards discovered something of H. P. B.'s extraordinary insight, I was not surprised to find that she had gauged accurately and unerringly my mental attitude on this my first visit, and it is an attitude which she never really discouraged. If those who talk so foolishly about her magnetising people could but know how she continually impressed upon us the absolute duty of proving all things and holding fast only to that which is good !

To go once was to go again, and so it came that after a few visits I began to see light. I caught glimpses of a lofty morality, of a self-sacrificing zeal, of a coherent philosophy of life, of a clear and definite science of man and his relation to a spiritual universe. These it was which attracted me—not phenomena, for I saw none. For the first time in my mental history I had found a teacher who could pick up the loose threads of my thought and satisfactorily weave them together, and the unerring skill, the vast knowledge, the loving patience of that teacher grew on me hour by hour. Quickly I learned that the so-called charlatan and trickster was a noble soul, whose every day was spent in unselfish work, whose whole life was pure and simple as a child's, who counted never the cost of pain or toil if these could advance the great cause to which her every energy was consecrated. Open as the day to a certain point, she was the incarnation of kindness—silent as the grave if need be, she was sternness personified at the least sign of faithlessness to the work which was her life. Grateful, so grateful for every affectionate attention, careless, so careless of all that concerned herself, she bound us to her, not simply as wise teacher, but as loving friend. Once I was broken down through long bodily and mental strain and the wheels of my life ran so heavily that they nearly stopped. Through it all her solicitude was untiring and one special proof of it that she gave, too personal to mention here, would have been thought of, perhaps, but by one in a million.

Perfect—no; faults—yes; the one thing she would hate most of all would be the indiscriminate praise of her personality. But when I have said that she was sometimes impetuous as a whirlwind, a very cyclone when she was really roused, I have told nearly all. And I have often thought it was more than possible that some of these outbursts were assumed for a special object. Lately they had almost vanished. Her enemies sometimes said she was rough and rude. We who knew her, knew that a more unconventional woman, in the very realest sense of the word, never lived. Her absolute indifference to all outward forms was a true indifference based upon her inner spiritual knowledge of the verities of the universe. Sitting by her when strangers came, as they did come from every corner of the earth, I have often watched with the keenest amusement their wonder at seeing a woman who always said what she thought. Given a prince and she would probably shock him, given a poor man and he would have her last shilling and her kindliest word.

How meagre all this is I know full well. Of the real H. P. B. we only caught occasional glimpses, and so necessarily we are thrown back on that human side of her life which appeals most to the human in us. Of her vast and profound knowledge this is not the time to speak, and if it were, how could one speak? Only its ripples ever reached us, but those would make an ordinary ocean. Probably we shall never know all the why and the wherefore of her recent incarnation. In 1889 Annie Besant and I were with her in France at the Forest of Fontainebleau, and while there she went over with us in manuscript part of the *Voice of the Silence*. Looking back on that time, I remember that the passages over which she was most impressive were those which describe the toilsome ascent of the pilgrim-soul. In the copy of the book which she gave me and which will never leave me, she has written, " To Herbert Burrows, my old friend in another and better incarnation, from his ever-loving H. P. B." It may be that in those words lie part of the key to the life that we knew.

Be that as it may, the real key for us is to be found in the example of her self-sacrificing devotion to her work. This is the note which was struck in the hearts of the hushed crowd who but yesterday gathered for the last time round the body of their loved teacher. That body has vanished from our sight, but the work remains. No great thought can ever die, no great effort for humanity can ever cease, but thought and effort can be accelerated by faithful service for mankind. More than ever now is that service needed, and they who would read aright the lesson of H. P. B.'s life will give that service unstintingly, ungrudgingly, if need be to the bitter end.

HERBERT BURROWS, F.T.S.

Teacher and Friend.

MY first acquaintance with Madame Blavatsky was in correspondence upon the subject of western occultism, during the year 1887.

I had often wished to see her, and had proposed to myself a way by which I could satisfy this desire, without in any way trespassing upon the slight acquaintance I had with the famous authoress of " Isis Unveiled ". Some months passed, and, for reasons in which a reclusive disposition found some sort of consolation, I had not yet seen Madame Blavatsky. I was in daily correspondence with members of the Theosophical Society, and others interested in the special subjects of its investigation, and every day the fact of my not having seen the chief mover in the occult renaissance of the 19th century, was growing more and more a source of annoyance to me. Quite unexpectedly, and to my intense satisfaction, the matter shaped itself. A letter from a London friend informed me that he had arranged for a few friends to meet at his house to discuss some of the problems in which we were mutually interested, and that if I would go up to town that evening, he would take me round to see " H.P.B." on the morrow.

I went—not to see my friends, nor to discuss problems, but—with the sole idea and purpose of seeing " H.P.B." That evening it seemed that Time stood still for the special purpose of laughing at my impatience. At last, however, the morning dawned and grew into a fine summer day, and towards noon I found myself with my friend at the house in Notting Hill, whence, he informed me, all the life of the Theosophical Society came. Entered, we were shown into the drawing-room, at least I presumed that was its appellation, though I have never seen, nor ever expect to see, another room like it. No, I was mistaken, for a few seconds later, in response to a familiar greeting from my friend, H.P.B. rose from her desk, where she had been hidden from view by an unusually large arm-chair, and came forward to receive us.

The largest and brightest blue eyes I have ever seen opened widely upon me as she took my hand and gave me welcome. All the confusion I had secretly predicted for myself fled from me on her first words. I felt at home and at ease with H.P.B. at once. " No, I will not be called ' Madame ', not by my best friend, there was nothing said of that when I was christened, and if you please I will be simply H.P.B. Have a seat there ; you smoke of course ; I'll make you a cigarette. E——, you flapdoodle, (this to my friend), if you can find my tobacco box on the place there, I'll mistake you for a gentleman." Then amid some laughter, as playful and buoyant as that of a child, she explained to me that E—— and she were " old friends " and that she was very fond of him, but that he often " took advantage of her old age and innocence ", and amid some repartee the tobacco was produced, and H.P.B. made cigarettes for each of us. Then we settled down to more serious talk, H.P.B. asking me about my studies in Theosophy and western occultism, and telling me of the success of the Theosophical movement, and how the people said this and that, and how the papers said much more, and that all were wrong because they did not understand, and had forgotten their history books and could not see where the movement was going to. And then she asked me to tell her about myself, and gave me some practical advice, and soon afterwards I had taken leave of the most interesting person that I had ever seen.

Such were the circumstances which led to my personal acquaintance with my beloved and revered teacher and friend. I was most pleasurably impressed with all that I had heard and seen during my brief visit to the home of the Theosophists, and the impression I most vividly recollect of H.P.B. herself, was of her surpassing kindliness of manner, her fearless candour, her remarkable vivacity, and above all the enthusiasm with which she spoke of the work which lay before the Theosophical Society. When, many months later, it was suggested that I should go to live at the London Headquarters, then in Lansdowne Road, I was only too glad to do so ; indeed I would have gone anywhere in order to have come more directly under the pure strong influence of H.P.B.'s example and teaching. The impressions I had first formed of her character remained unchanged during all my intimate association with her, until her passing away. In all my difficulties, whether in study or work, I have ever found her a wise counsellor and a strong guide. In sickness or sorrow she has always been kind, gentle, helpful and re-assuring ; in short, no one has ever filled my life in the double capacity of friend and teacher as she has done, and there is none to whom my gratitude so willingly flows.

I have said that H. P. B. was enthusiastic in her devotion to the cause which she had the honour of representing to the world. None who has had the privilege of working with H.P.B. could make any doubt upon this point. One of her first letters to me, phrased in her peculiar foreign way, informed me that "the first volume of my book (the *Secret Doctrine*) is from the press, and I am up since five o'clock these days". Her powers of endurance were equal in every respect to her great sense of devotion. She was an incessant worker. I have seen her at her desk as early as six o'clock in the morning, and often in the coldest days of the winter months, several sheets had passed under her pen before she took breakfast. Her application and tenacity were oftentimes a source of wonderment to me, especially when I considered that a great part of her life had been spent in the restless excitement of travel and adventure. Whatever may be the respective merits of the many Causes for which men and women have worked and died, certain it is that none have served them more fervently, persistently and painfully, than H. P. B. has served that of Theosophy. The night before her departure she was at her desk for a few minutes, effecting the last disposition of her papers; an editorial lay half-completed upon her desk, when for the last time she laid her pen aside to go to her passing rest. I was present at her departure, her right hand grew cold in mine. I will not attempt to describe my feelings when the consciousness of our loss, temporary though it may be, first dawned upon my mind. These moments of exquisite pain, when self-compassion, and a joy for the rest that had come to one I loved, tore my being in twain with their wild contest, will ever remain among the sacred memories of my life.

The last words from her pen were in defence of the truth for which she had lived; her dying lips framed words of encouragement to those upon whom the chief work would fall by her departure. What though many in the outside world have denied to her that honesty of purpose which they would be the first to claim for themselves, what though her untiring efforts in the cause of the Truth were repaid by the slanders and scoffs and sneers of the superficial crowd, and though her friendship was betrayed by the wounded vanity of a few fading personalities, yet she was unchecked in her purpose, and beyond the belief and desire of all her opponents, successful in the task she had undertaken in the face of such enormous discouragement. Those at least who lived with her, and best knew her, can tell how pure and unselfish was her whole nature, and how inspiring her teaching and her example. Nothing that I can say could add anything to the inherent beauty and purity of her character, and it is only with a feeling of grateful devotion and duty that I pen this feeble tribute to the memory of my greatest friend. WALTER R. OLD, F.T.S.

H. P. Blavatsky as seen through her Work.

HAVING joined the Theosophical Society in 1878, just as Madame Blavatsky and Col. Olcott were leaving America for India, and having followed the fortune of the Society ever since with increasing interest up to the time of H. P. B.'s death, it has occurred to me that the reasons that have led me, step by step, to the present time, may not be without interest to the readers of LUCIFER. It is not my purpose to write even an epitome of the Theosophical movement, or to attempt to show Madame Blavatsky's relations thereto, but rather to give a distant view of the teacher, as seen in her work, and show how her motive and aim may be discerned therefrom.

Coming to the T. S. doctrines from the orthodox protestant communion through familiarity with modern science, and philosophers like Herbert Spencer, these studies were immediately followed by mystical writers like Jacob Böhme, when at this point my attention was attracted to *Isis Unveiled*.

The result of all previous studies had been most unsatisfactory. The old religious creeds and theological interpretations of Christianity had been altogether repudiated ; and while the materialism into which modern science was obviously drifting was still less satisfactory, as giving the meaning of life, the nature and destiny of man, there lingered a feeling that there must be, after all, an element of truth and a beneficent purpose in the old religions. I was still earnestly searching for that which I had all along been unable to find, and yet which I felt must somewhere exist.

Two or three times I took up one of the volumes of *Isis*, only to lay it down, discouraged by the idea that I must read it through in order to know what it contained, and life at that time seemed very short, and time always precious. To " scan " these books hastily, and get, as I had often done with other volumes, a good general idea of their contents, seemed impossible. One day I opened the first volume, " Science ", and certain references therein to the Freemasons arrested my attention. I read on and on, and always with increasing interest. Before I had read to the end of the volume I began to hunt for some clue to the author. Who was " H. P. Blavatsky " ? I had found in the volumes certain references to a " Theosophical Society ". What was Theosophy, and what objects had the Society in view ? At last my interest became so great that I wrote a letter of enquiry to the publisher, Mr. Bouton, and the result was a most kind and courteous response from H. P. Blavatsky herself. A more specific letter of enquiry was followed by another kind answer, and by my joining the Society.

Soon after arriving in India H. P. B. wrote me again in regard to the *Theosophist*, just then getting out its first number and requested me to answer any attacks upon, or misrepresentations regarding the T.S. From that time till her residence at Avenue Road, she wrote me at considerable intervals of time and whenever occasion specially required.

Obtaining, from clues given in *Isis*, a more definite idea of that for which I had been so long in search, as also of its ear-marks in many directions, I soon learned the sign-manual of the true occultist, *viz.*, the absence of all egotism. As soon as I found a writer exploiting a doctrine for either personal fame or profit, I learned first to distrust, and finally to discard him. Applying this test to H. P. B., as I did from the beginning, I found her in the face of her immense knowledge never egotistic, and not only from every sign and all reliable information, free from all personal pride or ambition, but rejecting everything offered to herself in the way of adulation or revenue. If one called her great or wise, she replied, " I am but the servant of Masters who are indeed great ". Before leaving America she became a naturalized citizen of the U.S., and in doing so lost her pension from the Russian Government. The expense of founding the Society, of removing its headquarters to India, of starting the *Theosophist*, and of many other items, was largely borne by H. P. B. and Col. Olcott, while at the same time the small fees for dues, diplomas, etc., went in every instance into the treasury of the Society. I never knew her to solicit money in any way, even for the propaganda, and whenever presents of money were made to her they invariably went into the general fund of the Society.

I speak of these matters here, although so generally known, because as year after year went by, they furnished additional confirmation that here was no selfish egotist, no " adventuress ", but a worker for truth and for humanity who utterly sank herself in her work. This chain of evidence, beginning from the foundation of the Society and ending only at her last breath, is unbroken. Nor have I ever seen one particle of evidence to the contrary, though ignorant and unscrupulous persons have made all sorts of baseless and absurd charges against her.

I regard this line of evidence as of great importance for the reason that every other movement of modern times, claiming to work on similar lines, with which I am acquainted, and I know a good many personally and intimately, is open to the charge of exploitation for both money and personal aggrandisement. H. P. B. sometimes made the statement that some of these organizations had stolen the livery of Theosophy for the purpose of personal profit ; and in several instances, taking their professions at face-value with the reserved right of withdrawing if I found them other-wise, I joined them for the purpose of learning whether they were indeed true, and if they were working unselfishly on Theosophical lines. In every single instance their professions were false, and their boasted wisdom a delusion and a snare. One society was exploited by a convicted felon with great pretensions and manuscripts " borrowed " from the " literary remains " of P. B. Randolph. The test to which I referred in the early part of this paper is unfailing, and those who are inexperienced in such matters will do well to bear it in mind. The true teacher of arcane wisdom who really aims at the betterment of man is never egotistic, ambitious, mercenary, or time-serving. For fourteen years I have applied this test to H. P. B. with the result of confirming all my earlier impressions. She sacrificed fortune, fame, health, and at last life itself, for an *idea*, and that idea was first and last the teaching of the truths of Theosophy for the benefit of humanity.

Coming now to her teaching itself; those who have charged her followers—those who were glad to be taught and led by her—with foolish credulity or blind fanaticism, are invariably those who speak without knowledge, and malign without evidence.

If I examined her method and motive, I also critically examined the grounds of her knowledge, and the evidence of her statements. Every one who has ever read her larger works, even with curious and literary interest, has remarked the almost innumerable references to many books in many languages and written in almost every age. Profound, indeed, would be the knowledge and priceless the opportunity, of him who had the ability and the opportunity to verify all these references. He might, indeed, find here and there inaccuracies; what wonder, when these references were known to have been made *apparently* from memory, for it is well attested that she had a small number of volumes of any sort within her reach, and for months together never left the house in which she was living. Fortunately I have one of the largest libraries of occult and rare books to be found in America, and as my studies progressed I kept buying books to which she referred in *Isis*, in the *Secret Doctrine*, and in her almost number-less fugitive essays, for the purpose of verifying her statements as well as for further research. Through the clues thus afforded by her writings I was almost unconsciously gathering a mass of testimony in support of the old wisdom religion. Given, now, an . individual of fair intelligence, capable of estimating evidence, and loyal at all times to the simple truth, I could undertake to support the great bulk of H. P. B.'s teaching by outside and overwhelming testimony.

There is also another, and entirely different, line of evidence; I have already early in this paper referred to the Freemasons. It was at this point that I first became attracted to H. P. B.'s writings and joined the Society; I had been through thirty-two degrees of Masonry, and had here, as in the orthodox religions, found something wanting. There were, indeed, traditions of " Ancient Landmarks ", and that Masonry had originally been given to man " by God Himself ", but what these ancient land-marks really were, or how and when the G. A. of T. U. had revealed them to man was nowhere to be discovered.

In other words, there was the evidence of glyphics, and the meaning of symbolism ; and here my first real clue was derived from H. P. B. A friend of mine who has probably made more discoveries in the ancient Kabbala than anyone known to modern times, and who had devoted more than twenty years to this special line of work, raised once certain enquiries concerning his own researches, and expressed the doubt that any man then living could or would answer his enquiries. I suggested that he should write to H. P. B. in regard to the matter, and after some delay he did so. The result was nearly forty pages of very closely-written MSS. answering every question he had raised, and adding a fund of information that astonished the recipient beyond all measure. This gentleman is not and never has been a member of the T.S., but to the present time he declares his conviction that H. P. B. was the most profound and wonderful woman of this or of any age. He, a specialist for half a lifetime in an obscure and unknown field, found H. P. B. perfectly familiar with all his work.

But why multiply evidence on these lines so familiar to all who have really any knowledge of the subject of which I write ? If such methods of examination and such tests constantly applied for fourteen years constitute one a " blind follower " and an " unreasoning enthusiast ", then am I all that and more. Mine is not the pen to write a biography of H. P. B., nor to estimate the value and magnitude of her work. These are but brief personal reminiscences of one who never saw her, who could not, therefore, come under her personal magnetism, nor be in any way prejudiced by personal contact. From the beginning I have measured the work of H. P. B. *by itself*, as well as by every available test and comparison, and allowed it to stand or fall on its merit. The time has now come when every one at all interested in the teachings and work of the T. S. must apply this discriminating method, and if the student be in real earnest and ready to accord to truth its own intrinsic value the result can be in nowise uncertain. There is no record of any such teacher in the western world since our boasted " civilization " emerged from barbarism.

If it be just to judge a tree by its fruit, a character by its service to humanity, and a personality by its self-forgetfulness, then will H. P. Blavatsky soon be recognised in her true character, and placed among the benefactors of humanity.

Her mission remains to the Society she came forth to found. If its members have not apprehended her mission, then, indeed, have they studied in vain, and she hath imagined a vain thing. Those who have received most through larger opportunity and from personal contact with the teacher, have the larger duty.

> " Nay, O thou candidate for Nature's hidden lore !
> If one would follow in the steps of holy Tathâgata,
> Those gifts and powers are not for Self."

But what if the disciple prove forgetful and untrue, and wander off in search of Self ? The teachings still remain, and truer disciples yet will come to carry on her work. A tidal wave raised by her hand has already swept around the world. Its pulses throb in every artery of life. The Society has but to feed the body already transfused with a newer life, to keep it intact as a whole, and to draw from exhaustless sources already in their keeping, to move the world, as it has not been moved for many a weary century. *The nucleus of a Universal Brotherhood* is already formed. Shall this Laya-centre lift humanity and enlighten the world? H. P. B. is not dead. There is no death. H. P. B. has diffused her life into the Theosophical Society, bidding them again diffuse its vital stream to every soul that breathes; adding their life-force to hers, and so to *pass it on*, involving all; enlightening all; redeeming all from selfishness and sin. " Death " was her most heroic deed. It marks and means renewed life. Hitherto we have received, now we must give. Hitherto we have learned; now, like her, we must teach. The harvest is ready, and the reapers are *not* a few, and the golden grain shall not fall back into the ground, nor be devoured by the beasts of the fields and the fowls of the air, for an innumerable host that no man can number stand hungry and waiting without. They are waiting without, foot-sore and weary with life. They have waited long, clamouring for bread, and receiving only a stone, and here is the *One only Truth* that can feed and satisfy the starving soul; the one truth that to the last analysis can satisfy the reasoning mind, and give new life and hope to the sorrowing heart of humanity. *Let us push on the work of H. P. B.*

J. D. BUCK, F.T.S.

The Opinion of a Hindu about H.P.B.

[*The subjoined Paper was not published in January, because H. P. B. was the Editor of* LUCIFER; *I print it here now, among the many testimonies to her great worth.*—ED.]

IN perusing the article headed, " The Theosophical Society and H.P.B.", by Mrs. A. Besant in the December number of LUCIFER, I was struck with several things, and although I cannot fully express my mind on all that I think and know about the subject, I yet feel myself constrained to speak a few words on it.

There is not the least doubt that H. P. B. is a woman of mysterious and wonderful occult powers, and must have acquired them, I believe, with great, very great difficulty and drawbacks; for now-a-days it is very rare to find out, *i.e.*, to recognise, a powerful Yogi in India, and especially to succeed in getting anything out of him; the more so by a woman born of Mlecha tribe. That, however, somehow or other—hcw, it is more than I can say—she has succeeded in getting the key of the true Hindu and therefore of the subsequent Buddhistic Secret Philosophy, there can be no question, no doubt and no hesitation about it. Those who really understand anything about the sublime and mysterious philosophy of the Hindus—including the Hindus themselves—can at once find out what she knows and what she is ; it does not require the demonstration of her occult powers to convince such a person. A few words on the real point, nay, only one word and the sign of a particular place, and he knows at once what she is.

I am not known to the Theosophical Society in India, England, or America, although I know H. P. B. very well. I am not a Russian, an Englishman, or an American, and therefore I have no earthly reason to speak well or ill of a person, unless I am thoroughly convinced of the one thing or the other. Add to this the fact that I am a Hindu and a Brahmin of the high caste, and then you will be able to judge what motive can have actuated me, *except truth*, in speaking one word in favour of a person who, I must say, does not do justice to the philosophy of my ancestors, by reveal-ing it to the *Ausoon* of the West, who are every inch Mlecha, in spite of all their vaunted civilisation and modern science.

Those who call H. P. B. " a fraud " are much mistaken, they do not know her. I would be glad to give up everything I have in this world to become such a fraud, if anybody will come forward to teach me. Is it not sufficient for the Westerns to know that a proud Brahmin, who knows not how to bend his body before any mortal being in this world, except his superiors in relation or religion, joins his hands like a submissive child before the white *Yogini* of the West ? Why so ? because she is no longer a Mlecha woman ; she has passed that stage ; and every Hindu—the purest of the pure amongst the Brahmins—would be proud and delighted to call her Hindu and a mother—there is no doubt about it. India cannot forget her, has not forgotten her, and the Hindus will, at no distant time, get their *Yogini* back to their house. They may be careless and ignorant, but they are certainly not ungrateful or faithless, like most of the civilised people of the West. I am really very sorry for the conduct of some of my mistaken countrymen, during the Coulomb farce on the missionary stage in India, who for fear of disclosing the names of the Yogis to the people of the West, lost no time in concealing the fact, so as to make it appear that there were no real Yogis in India at all. I myself certainly do not like the idea of publish-ing the Secret Philosophy of the East for the information of the people of the West, who have nothing but contempt and hatred for everything called Eastern, and especially Indian ; there may be very, very few exceptions to these ; but there is one consolation in this ; that those books are dead letters for the *Saheb loks* unless fully explained, and H. P. B. is the only person who can explain them in the West. But I sincerely hope that she will not abuse her authority, unless with the consent of those from whom she received.   As a Brahmin, I would always object, and I consider it my duty to do so, to the publishing of the secret sublime Truths of my religion and ancestors, especially amongst the people whose food is beef, who drink spirituous liquors, and have beds composed of spring cushions made of down and feathers.* It is very easy to envy the powers possessed by others, and to wish to possess the same; but it is very, very difficult to attain these, more difficult than I am able to express.

Rai B. K. Laheri, F.T.S.

How an Agnostic saw Her.

FROM stale, grey London we were whirled out among the green fields and through masses of fruit trees white as the vesture of Soracte's† hill, that day we followed to the furnace the mortal remains of Helena Petrovna Blavatsky.   Away we were whirled through plains grazed by fat oxen that would have made a holocaust worthy to have celebrated the victory of Platæa, and through a gloomy plantation of resinous pine that would have made a funeral pyre for Patroclus.   And, from among the bushes, the birds sang as merrily as they did erst in Eden, and the primroses prinkt the green slopes as fragrantly and daintily as in the old romantic days, when they bore up the dancing feet of Titania and Oberon beneath the light of the moon.

And on we sped with our dead through that blue-skied afternoon in the month of May.   We bore no warrior to the pyre.   We needed no oxen and resinous pine.   We hasted to a mortuary furnace more intense than ever reddened the heavens round Ilium, or rendered Gehenna hideous with unctuous smoke and the odour of smouldering bones.

We were accompanying to the flames an oracle, a sphinx, or a sibyl, rather than anything that the world commonly produces in its ordinary villages and towns.   We accompanied the remains of what erst was the madcap girl of Ekaterinoslow, who, with nuptial withes, had, as a freak, tied her wild and impetuous young heart to that of tame and frosty age; and had since, in every realm of this planet of ours, thought and toiled and suffered, and had been misunderstood and calumniated.   She felt her strength, and knew the weakness of the chattering imbeciles that, in the census-return, make up the millions of a country's population.   Mabel Collins tells the truth when she says that Madame Blavatsky had a contempt for mankind; but forgets to say that it was an affectionate contempt.

---

* A true Hindu would never care for the Western civilisation which, like an onion, only emits a strong smell of a peculiar kind, too much provocative of passion, and discloses no substance when the several skins are taken off.

† *Vide* Hor., Ode ix.

She was neither pessimist nor misanthropist. She was simply an upright a nd romantically honest giantess, who measured herself with the men and women with whom she came in contact, and felt the contrast, and was not hypocrite enough to pretend she did not feel it. But she did not call even those who reviled and wronged her by a more bitter epithet than " flapdoodles ". Such assailants as even the Coulombs and Dr. Coues she referred to with expressions equivalent to " Father, forgive them, for they know not what they do ", even when these assailants were doing their best to cut her, soul and body, with numerous and ghastly wounds, and to fill them with salt and salve them with vitriol.

She had no more rancour against the " flapdoodles " than I have against my butt, " Mr. John Smith, nonconformist and cheesemonger "; and my ill-will t owards him is shown by my working away for him year after year barring up my path to literary renown and worldly success, and becoming prematurely blind and grey-haired, wrinkled and old, for his sake. If Madame Blavatsky, like every other ambitious man and woman, had flattered the " flapdoodles " and catered to their prejudices, they would have paid her for her services and awarded her the kind of excellently stale character that would obtain one a situation as a Methodist preacher. But she was not one of the Methodist preacher type, and they give her a character (*vide* Coues and others) that would obtain for the very devil a more exalted position in hell. She declined to place her feet in the very marks in which Mrs. Grundy trod, even as an eagle could not be made to walk for leagues on the hoof-prints of an ass. She at one time amused some gapers and gazers with specimens of ho me-made " miracles "; and these " miracles ", light as a game at Nap, they elected to associate with Theosophy, which, compared with a frivolous game at Nap, is serious as the cannonading at Trafalgar. They judged her on the testimony of a snake she had warmed in her bosom, a Madame Coulomb, a renegade friend, the most venomous viper the world knows of, especially if the viper be a female one. And on the coilings and wrigglings and hissings of this adder they are mean enough and mediocre enough to base devilish aspersions against the strong, brave, and simple woman with the remains of whom we travel on to the furnace at Woking. Such was the tenour of my contemplations by the way.

One in a wagon-load of uncraped mourners, I reached the crematorium. It is a red-brick building, which, in appearance, seems a mongrel between a chapel, a tile-kiln and a factory chimney. You enter by a mortuary chapel, passing through which you emerge through heavy folding doors of oak, and find yourself in an apartment, in the middle of the floor of which, and end to you, there is a great iron object like the boiler of a locomotive, but supported by and embedded in masonry. The Theosophists crowd round this boiler-looking object with anxious but decorous curiosity, to gratify which one of the attendants turned, on the end of the object, an iron snib which left a circular orifice about the size of a crown piece. Those present looked in succession into this opening ; most, I noticed, gave one quick glance, and turned away with an involuntary shudder. When it came to my turn to peep in I wondered not that my predecessors had shuddered. If Virgil or Milton or Dante had ever seen such an Inferno, they would never have written about the Inferno at all, relinquishing the theme as utterly ineffable. Inside that furnace was filled with towels of fire whisked by the arm of the very devil himself. I can look on a common furnace ; but I shall never again peep through that iron eye-let into the viscera of hell.

As I was so contemplating, the hearse arrived and drew up on the gravel in front of the door of the mortuary chapel. Into the chapel the coffin was borne and laid upon an oaken tressel, and we all stood up and uncovered. The coffin was literally laden with and hidden in flowers, and a heavy perfume pervaded the air. Under those flowers lay the mortal remains of her who was dear to all of us, and had wielded a personal influence such as mere mediocrity, however amiable, could never have exercised. The *glamour* with which she evoked towards herself human respect and affection was a greater " miracle " than any her traducers have drawn our attention to. It was equalled only by the envenomed hate towards her with which she could apparently inspire her enemies. And how she could have enemies at all is a " miracle " to me ; for, in spite of her tremendous attainments and unrivalled talent, she had not a vestige of pedantic assumption, and had the simple heart of a child. " Impostor " indeed ! She was almost the only mortal I have ever met who was *not* an impostor. And the flagrant and apparent ignorance of those who style her so is contemptible. They allege that she " founded a new religion ". Where and when did either she or hers make such claim ? On the authority of mendacious popular gossip, they allege that the " new religion " like the baleful old mockery of a religion that is in this country, by law established, was attested by thaumaturgy and miracle. They are ignorant of the very elements of Theosophy who make such a charge. Even if you were to take it for granted that, by a clever juggle, Madame Blavatsky found a tea-cup under the ground and mystically mended a trayful of broken china, the fact would have no more connection with Theosophy than Tenterden Church has with the Goodwin Sands, or lawn tennis with Christianity. Ye sneerers of cheap sneers, read " Isis Unveiled ", " The Secret Doctrine ", and the " Key to Theosophy ", and you will find that Theosophy is, most likely, something too high for your comprehension, but something that is immeasurably removed from the possibility of being assisted by the legerdemain of a charlatan or the jugglery of a mountebank.

Mr. G. R. S. Mead, a young gentleman of refined features and much *spirituelle* of expression, stepped forward to the head of the coffin of her to whom he had been private secretary and attached friend. There, in the most solemn hush, he read an impressive address impressively. As his

4

silvery voice rose and fell in melancholy cadence, I was wafted away as in a vision to the glen where—

> "In accents soft and calm,
> Kilmahoe gave out the psalm,"

among the heathery hills of my own loved land, to sterner and less literate heretics who were persecuted with fire and steel, even as the heretics among whom I now stood were persecuted with sneering and calumny.

But, while thus musing, the door from the crematorium into the chapel opened, and four employés, who did not look exactly like either stokers or butchers, but had some resemblance to each, entered, and, in a business-like manner, went two to each end of the tressel, and, raising it by its four handles, moved off with it through the doorway. Four Theosophists who had known and loved Madame Blavatsky, and had, like myself, found the grandest and the worst-abused woman in the world identical, followed her remains through that wide doorway down to the furnace. The mass of flowers wafted us another wealth of fragrance as they disappeared, and the great doorway was slammed and bolted with a decisive mastery suggestive of the fall of the portcullis in Hades.

Tressel, coffin, and flowers had gone. They were now behind that inexorable door, as also the mortal remains of the strongest, bravest, and noblest woman that shall ever grasp this poor trembling hand, all too mean and weak to write her obsequies. " Give up thy life if thou wouldst live..... Before he cast his shadow off his mortal coil, that pregnant course of anguish and illimitable pain, in him will men a great and holy Buddha honour......When to the Permanent is sacrificed the mutable, the prize is thine : the drop returneth whence it came. The OPEN PATH leads to the changeless change—Nirvâna, the glorious state of Absoluteness, the Bliss past human thought."*

Since Madame Blavatsky's arrival in England the Theosophic movement has made steady progress, principally among the influential and educated ; for, like Positivism, it offers no haven of mental indolence and moral lethargy for the unlettered and unthinking. The most notable English convert is Mrs. Annie Besant, whom we always predicted would, in time, relinquish the cold *this-worldism* of the Secularist.

Anyone with the capacity to recognise human greatness and to discern the *Shekinah* light of Genius—and this is written by one who has looked in the face of Carlyle—could not fail to know that the world held only one Madame Blavatsky. There was a charm in the sublime simplicity of her manner which drew her followers to her as the horse-shoe magnet attracts the steel filings. She struck you as a square-headed, rough-featured, stout, carelessly-draped, Oliver Cromwell-looking personage, as you sat alone with her over coffee and smoking with her cigarettes of her own making ;

---

* " The Voice of the Silence," translated and annotated by H. P. Blavatsky.

but she had that overflow of soul which falls to the lot of few, and such as might, but for superior mental fibre and balance, have impelled her, like Wiertz and Blake, to ride on steeds of fire while the multitude deemed their genius dashed with madness. Hers had been a life of storm, toil, and unrest, which had left their autographs written cruelly upon her face, and had originated or accentuated incurable illness. She kept herself among us by taking doses of arsenic which would have killed the strongest. And yet she was cheerful and sociable, incapable of an ungenerous thought, and she had not a mean drop of blood in her veins.

Her manners and mode and matter of speech were far too unconventional for the drawing-room. She could use expressions of expletive force which are compatible with dashing dragoons rather than with simpering dudes. She had that tremendous strength of idiosyncrasy which can dispense with receiving lessons in deportment from the dancing-master. The feeble yew looks best when clipped and pruned; but the forest oak appears to most advantage in the possession of the full length and strength of his great arms with which he has grappled with the roaring storm.

Theosophy or no Theosophy, the most extraordinary woman of our century, or of any century, has passed away. Yesterday the world had one Madame Blavatsky—to-day it has none. The matrix of heredity environment in which she was moulded has been broken. Through the coming ages of time or eternity shall the shattered fragments of that matrix be gathered up and refixed, and another Helena Petrovna Hahn be born upon the earth, when the earth is sane enough not to misunderstand her, to persecute her, and seek to bury her name in a cataclysm of falsehood, hatred, and slander?

Any discriminating person who came in contact with her could easily understand why she was so dearly loved, and no less easily conjecture why she was so bitterly hated. She wore her heart upon her sleeve. Unfortunately for anyone who hopes to " get on " in this world, she did not possess even a single rag of the cloak of hypocrisy. She rattled away rather than conversed upon persons and principles in merry sarcasm and happy cynicism, but, to those who could understand her, without even a suspicion of bitterness or malevolence. She had none of that restrained precision in utterance in regard to friends and contemporaries which ladies in society adopt. She meant no ill, and so it did not occur to her that she could speak any evil. She was, if you like, too simple and ingenuous and straightforward; she wanted in discretion; she was entirely lacking in hypocrisy; and thus she became an easy butt for the envenomed arrows of her traducers.

Now, through dark death and the crematorium fire, she has passed from among us, ye slanderers. Apart from the nobility of her soul and the magnitude of her achievements, I cherish dearly the memory of one I loved, of a misunderstood one whom I understood, and one of the very few who ever understood me. The mystery to which we are passing may be the richer for her presence ; but this mediocre world of ours is all the poorer for her loss. Her demise falls heavily upon me who was of her brotherhood, but who do not share in the stoical consolations of her creed.

To her followers she is still alive. The Madame Blavatsky I knew " can in the mind of no Theosophist be confounded with the mere physical instrument which served it for but for one brief incarnation ". But I lay not firm enough hold upon this doctrine for it to give consolation to me. The Madame Blavatsky I knew is *dead* to me. Of course, all that might be permanent or impermanent of her still whirls in the vortex of the universe ; but she lives to me only as do others on the roll of the good and great, by the halo of her memory and the inspiration of her example. Her followers are gnostic on grave issues of teleology on which I am only agnostic. They have unbroken communion with their dead ; but I am left to mourn. It is not for me to altogether overleap the barriers of sense, and, by the divine light of spiritual perception, behold help extended to me from that awful bourne from which no traveller returns. To me Madame Blavatsky is dead, and another shadow has fallen athwart my life, which has never had much sunshine to bless it.

SALADIN.
(In *Agnostic Journal*.)

———————

H. P. B. at Enghien.

IN the spring of 1884 H. P. B. was staying in Rue Notre Dame des Champs, Paris, and in the house were living Col. Olcott, Mohini M. Chatterji and the writer. Part of the time Bertram Keightley was also there. As always since I have known H. P. B. during the past seventeen years, she was there as elsewhere engaged daily with her writing, save for an occasional drive or visit. Many visitors from all classes were constantly calling, and among the rest came the Countess d'Adhémar, who at once professed a profound admiration for H. P. B. and invited her to come to the Château owned by the Count at Enghien, just outside the city, including in her invitation myself and Mohini Chatterji. Bertram Keightley was also invited for a few days. The invitation was accepted and we all went out to Enghien, where H. P. B. was given two large rooms downstairs and the others slept in rooms on the upper floors. Every convenience was given to our beloved friend, and there she continued her writing, while I at her request carefully read over, sitting in the same room, *Isis Unveiled*, making indices at the foot of each page, as she intended to use it in preparing the *Secret Doctrine*.

A lake was at one side of the house and extensive grounds covered with fine timber hid the building from the road, part being a well kept fruit and flower garden. A slight description of the rooms is necessary. Wide stairs led up to the hall; on one side, which we may call the road front, was the billiard room, the high window of which opened upon the leaden roof of the porch; the dining room looked out at the back over the edge of the lake, and the drawing room opened from it on the other side at right angles to the side of the billiard room. This drawing room had windows opening on three sides, so that both garden and lake could be seen from it. In it was the grand piano at the end and side opposite the dining room door, and between the two side windows was a marble slab holding ornaments; between the windows, at the end near the piano, was the fireplace, and at that corner was one of the windows giving a view of the lake. Every evening it was the custom to spend some time in the drawing room in conversation, and there, as well as in the dining room, took place some phenomena which indeed were no more interesting than the words of H. P. B., whether those were witty, grave or gay. Very often Countess d'Adhémar's sister played the piano in a manner to delight even H. P. B., who was no mean judge. I remember well one melody, just then brought out in the world of Paris, which pleased her immensely, so that she often asked for its repetition. It was one suggestive of high aspiration and grandiose conceptions of nature. Many lively discussions with the Count on one side and H. P. B. on the other had place there, and often in the very midst of these she would suddenly turn to Mohini and myself, who were sitting listening, to repeat to us the very thoughts then passing in our brains.

Count d'Adhémar did not ask for the production of phenomena, but often said that could he and a few of his friends be convinced about Theosophy perhaps much good would result in France. Some of us desired in our hearts that in the home of such kind friends phenomena might occur, but none suggested it to H. P. B. But one day at dinner, when there were present the Count and Countess, their son Raoul, H. P. B., Mohini, the Countess' sister, myself, and one other, the strong and never-to-be-forgotten perfume which intimate friends of H. P. B. knew so well as often accompanying phenomena or coming of itself, floated round and round the table, plainly perceptible to several and not perceived either before or afterwards. Of course many sceptics will see nothing in this, but the writer and others well know that this of itself is a phenomenon, and that the perfume has been sent for many miles through the air as a message from H. P. B. or from those hidden persons who often aided in phenomena or in teachings. At this dinner, or at some other during the visit, we had all just come in from the flower garden. I had plucked a small rosebud and placed it upon the edge of the tumbler between myself and the Countess' sister who was on my left, H. P. B. being seated on my right. This lady began to talk of phenomena, wondering if H. P. B. could do as related of the Indian yogis. I replied that she could if she would, but did not ask her, and added that she could make even that small rosebud bloom at once. Just then H. P. B. stretched her hand out towards the rose, not touching it, and said nothing, continuing at once her conversation and the dinner. We watched the bud until the end of the meal and saw that it grew in that space of time much larger and bloomed out into a rose nearly full grown.

On another evening after we had all been in the drawing room for some time, sitting without lights, the moon shining over the lake and all nature being hushed, H. P. B. fell into a thoughtful state. Shortly she rose and stood at the corner window looking over the water, and in a moment a flash of soft light shot into the room and she quietly smiled. Reminding me of this evening the Countess d'Adhémar writes in this month of June :—

" H. P. B. seemed wrapped in thought, when suddenly she rose from her chair, advanced to the open window, and raising her arm with a commanding gesture, faint music was heard in the distance, which advancing nearer and nearer broke into lovely strains and filled the drawing room where we were all sitting. Mohini threw himself at H. P. B.'s feet and kissed the hem of her robe, which action seemed the appropriate outcoming of the profound admiration and respect we all felt toward the wonderful being whose loss we will never cease to mourn."

This astral music was very plain to us all, and the Count especially remarked upon its beauty and the faintness of it as it sank away into the unknown distance. The whole house was full of these bell sounds at night when I was awake very late and others had retired. They were like signals going and coming to H. P. B.'s room downstairs. And on more than one occasion as we walked in the grounds under the magnificent trees, have they shot past us, sometimes audible to all and again only heard by one or two.

The lead roof of the portico was a place where after dinner we sometimes sat, and there on some of those delightful evenings we were joined by the Countess Wachtmeister, who afterwards did so much for the comfort of H. P. B. at Würzburg and other places. Many chats were held there about occultism. In one of these we were speaking of images in the Astral Light and H. P. B. said : " Well, you know that it moves as other things in Kosmos do, and that the time comes when it floats off, as it were, letting another mass of the same ' light ' take its place ".

It was with a feeling of some regret that we left this delightful place where such quiet reigned and where H. P. B. was able to work amid the beauty and the stillness of nature. It cannot be blotted from the memory, because there our friend and teacher was untroubled by the presence of curiosity seekers, and thus was free to present to us who believed in her a side of her many-sided nature which pleased, instructed and elevated us all.

One incident remains to be told for which we must depend on others. I took away with me a book which could not be finished there, and just before leaving France went out to Enghien to return it. There I met the Countess d'Adhémar, who said that the peculiar and unmistakable perfume of which I spoke above had come in the house after we had all left. It was one evening about two days after H. P. B.'s departure and the d'Adhémars had some friends to dinner. After dinner they all went into the drawing room and soon noticed the perfume. It came, as they said to me, in rushes, and at once they began to hunt it out in the room, coming at last to the marble slab described, where, from one spot in the stone, they found the perfume rushing out in volumes. Such was the quantity of it that, as the Countess said to me, they were compelled to open the windows, since the odour was overpowering in large masses. In returning to Paris I told H. P. B. of this and she only said : " It sometimes happens ".

WILLIAM Q. JUDGE, F.T.S.

In Memoriam.

THE first occasion on which I ever heard of H. P. B. was on reading Mr. Sinnett's *Occult World*, at the close of 1883-1884. At that time I had, with other friends in Cambridge, been studying the phenomena of spiritualism to a slight extent, and had also been reading all the books on magic which I could find in the University Library. Consequently the ideas did not come to me in an entirely new fashion, and Madame Blavatsky was less associated with the *Occult World* phenomena in my mind than with the letters which are printed in that work. It was in the spring of 1884 that I first saw her. I was then on the eve of joining the T.S., or had just done so, and was attending a meeting of the London Lodge held in Lincoln's Inn, for the purpose of settling, under the presidency of Col. Olcott, certain differences between the Oriental and Occidental views on Theosophy. During that meeting I noticed particularly a somewhat stout lady quietly enter the room and sit down near the door. Nothing occurred till some mention was made of what Madame Blavatsky had done, when this lady remarked quietly, " That's so ", after which a general rush was made towards her, and she was carried off to the head of the room, while the meeting broke up in confusion. It appeared that Madame Blavatsky had found it imperatively necessary to attend that meeting ; had started from Paris without luggage or attendant ; had in fact arrived by the mail train and had followed her occult instinct in guiding herself to the rooms where the meeting was being held, of which she had not the address. As Madame Blavatsky returned to Paris the next day or the day after, I had no opportunity of making her acquaintance. When next I saw her she was staying at the house of Mrs. Arundale, in Elgin Crescent. I cannot say that, beyond admiring her learning very greatly, I was very closely drawn to her. Outside the fact that I was a member of the T.S.

and anxious to get information, there was nothing in me to draw her attention. I was then in the midst of my medical studies, and, living outside London, had very little time to spend in visits. It was during the autumn, however, that Madame Blavatsky, together with my friends Mr. and Mrs. Cooper-Oakley, rented rooms in Victoria Road, and I there joined them for a short time previous to their departure for India. Even under such favourable circumstances I cannot lay claim to being intimate with her. So far as I could tell, I was to her the friend of Mr. and Mrs. Cooper-Oakley, with whom she might talk and chat in the evening when her work for the day was done, and nothing more. I may, I think, lay claim to the proud distinction that of all who had at that time lived in the same house with Madame Blavatsky, I was alone in never having witnessed any of the phenomena which were so frequently seen in her neighbourhood. I saw the steamer leave the docks on the Mersey, and did not see Madame Blavatsky again till 1887, when I twice visited her at Ostende. In the meantime I had of course seen and read all that was to be heard of the S.P.R. Investigation. I was present at the meetings at which the report was read, and most certainly it made very little impression on my mind. I had been reading a good many " detective stories ", and I well remember the poor impression as a story which the report made on me. As to the rest immediately concerning Madame Blavatsky, I knew her learning, wit, and cleverness. I thoroughly believed in the existence of the Masters as constituting a necessary link in human evolution, and the only effect on my mind was a still greater contempt for circumstantial evidence, hearsay reports, and working hypotheses. Theosophy was itself; Madame Blavatsky had brought it to the world, and I felt a trust in facts as opposed to appearances.

However, it was in 1887 that I was first brought in close contact with H. P. B. She was then in Ostende, engaged in writing the *Secret Doctrine*. At the time Theosophy seemed to be slowly decaying as a force in England, and together with other friends I felt that some strong step had to be taken. Consequently, after corresponding, Madame Blavatsky replied that if she found that the desire for her presence was sufficiently strong, she was willing to leave her retirement and come to London to help on the work. All of us wrote to her and finally she consented to come. At Ostende I found Madame Blavatsky and the Countess Wachtmeister living together, and was at once set to work to read some part of the *Secret Doctrine*. Almost directly on my return to London, I heard that H. P. B. had been taken suddenly ill and that her life was in danger. A slight chill had developed dangerous symptoms which by some extraordinary means disappeared, and she recovered a second time from a condition in which recovery is rarely, if ever known.

It can easily be imagined, then, that on my second visit to assist in her journey to England, I was to the last degree dismayed to find the day when we were compelled to leave damp and foggy, and that a thin misty rain was falling. It must be remembered that Madame Blavatsky had not set foot outside her rooms, she would not come out of her private room into the parlour if the window was open, and as a rule her own room was nearly unbearable to others from the heat which made it pleasant to her. However, we started and got on board the steamer with ease ; the tide was full, and the steamer lay alongside the wharf at a convenient height. But Dover ! There the tide was low, and many were the damp and dripping steps up which we had to climb. However, a carrying chair and porters overcame the difficulty. But her face, as she was being carried up, was a study. Imagine the circumstances, recollect Madame Blavatsky's face, and the scene is easily conjured up. Next came an even greater difficulty, crippled as her limbs were from disuse—the getting her into the railway carriage from the low platform. However, an end comes to everything, and so it did to the journey, and she arrived safe and well at Norwood in the evening, and, further, there were no ill effects to be detected next day.

We settled down to work at Maycot, Bertram Keightley and myself, with H. P. B., her maid, and one servant, staying there till September through the heat of the Jubilee summer. Work was the order of the day, and its results are visible. A great deal of the *Secret Doctrine* was written again ; it was corrected and recorrected and type-written, LUCIFER was started, and the Blavatsky Lodge was formed. Friends gathered around her and rallied to the Theosophical flag. Then came the time for expansion, for the Countess Wachtmeister was on the point of arrival, and another exodus was made to Lansdowne Road. Unintermittently the work went on, and the focus of activity steadily extended its rays, until the present condition of affairs was reached.

Thus it may be seen that for at least two years I was closely associated on intimate terms with Madame Blavatsky. It is next to impossible to convey to one who did not know her the varied sides of her personal character. To those who were merely curious about her and her work she was courteous and external, but it was not until the interest in Theosophy became real that H. P. B. showed herself as she was. Well do those who love her know that almost every fault and sin imaginable in human character have been assigned to her. Doubtless to the external and carnal observer some colour may have been given, and even then we know that nature is not all smiles and that thunder-showers clear the air. But what I distinctly affirm is that such excuses are not valid. It is not in any degree possible to comprehend the many phases of a single human character, and especially such a complex one as H. P. B. I am positive from long observation of her actions that there was a purpose in all her acts and words, and that it depended on the observers how much they might profit by the lesson. This may sound ridiculous to some, but I con-vinced myself that H. P. B. used the physical instrument which was called

H. P. Blavatsky with distinct, untiring purpose, although the instrument grew so impaired by sickness that it became increasingly difficult to direct it.

To all who assisted her work she was ever ready to give counsel and help, and only those who received her help can appreciate it at its just value. But though they feel it, they cannot talk of it, for it is not possible to bring the deepest feelings to the surface. Personally, as I know her, I may say that I found in her the wise teacher, the loving friend who knew how to cut for the purpose of curing, and an example in practice when the need arose of how to regulate action to theosophical ideas. I may close by saying that I regard myself as most fortunate in the Karma which brought me in association with H. P. B. and enabled me to assist so far as I could in the work of the lion-hearted leader of the Cause of Theosophy.

ARCH. KEIGHTLEY, M.B., F.T.S.

H. P. Blavatsky and her Mission.

H. P. BLAVATSKY is dead, but the great soul that was embodied in her form, still lives. The woman, called " the Sphinx of the nineteenth century", because she was understood only by a few, has given up the ghost; but the great soul, the *Maha Atma*, dwelling within that mortal form and using it as an instrument for shedding rays of spiritual light into this era of mental darkness, has only left its habitation, and returned to a more congenial home, to rest from its labours.

It is doubtful whether there ever was any great genius and saviour of mankind, whose personality while upon this earth, was not misunderstood by his friends, reviled by his enemies, mentally tortured and crucified, and finally made an object of fetish-worship by subsequent generations. H. P. B. seems to be no exception to the rule. The world, dazzled by the light of her doctrines, which the majority of men did not grasp, because they were new to them, looked upon her with distrust, and the representatives of scientific ignorance, filled with their own pomposity, pronounced her to be " the greatest impostor of the age", because their narrow minds could not rise up to a comprehension of the magnificence of her spirit. It is, however, not difficult to prophesy, that in the near future, when the names of her enemies will have been forgotten, the world will become alive to a realisation of the true nature of the mission of H. P. B., and see that she was a messenger of Light, sent to instruct this sinful world, to redeem it from ignorance, folly and superstition, a task which she has fulfilled as far as her voice was heard and her teachings accepted.

Then will the historian of those times ransack the archives for the purpose of finding some bit of history of the life of H. P. B., and unless all the vilifications that have been written about her have found their way to the pile of manure from which they emanated, it is not impossible that her memory may then be besmirched by scribblers of the future, in the same way as the memory of Cagliostro, Theophrastus Paracelsus, and other great souls, has been besmirched by irresponsible scribblers of the present time. It is for this and for other self-evident reasons very desirable that something reliable in regard to the life of H. P. B. should be published by some competent person having been well acquainted with her, and being not a worshipper of personalities, but capable of studying and describing the life of the inner man. The true life of every spiritually awakened human being is not his external but his interior life. To describe merely the events that took place in the earth-life of an embodied genius and not to paint his interior life, his thoughts and feelings, is to describe merely the history of the house which that genius inhabited during its earthly career and to take no notice of the inhabitant. Thus even the best written account of the life of H. P. B., that has been published, resembles a painting of a bird of paradise after the bird has been stripped of its plumage and dressed for the kitchen. It is the treatment of a highly poetical subject with a careful avoidance of all poetry. But the feathers of a bird are as much an essential part of the bird as its muscles and bones, and the poetical and ideal part of a man is a more essential thing in his nature than the structure of his physical body or the cut of his coat. It is H. P. B.'s inner life, her mode of thinking and feeling, that is of importance and ought to be understood ; all the rest belongs to external things that are not worthy the attention of the true occultist.

Each person has a double nature, an external and an internal life, and H. P. B. formed no exception to that rule. She was neither wholly earthly nor wholly divine.

Some poet says :

> Two natures are within each human being :
> One is a child of the clear light of day.
> In it is nothing dark, but all is seeing,
> There is all sunshine, nothing hid away.
> Its innermost thy eye may penetrate,
> There is no secret and no mystery ;
> In it rule wisdom, justice, love and faith :
> Spotless as crystal is its purity.
>
> The other is a being born of night,
> Fill'd with dark clouds that change and change again.
> It baffles reason and ignores the light :
> It is a stranger in its own domain.
> Intangibly it fills our daily life
> With mocking goblins ; its discordant reign
> Begetting errors and discordant strife :
> Tangling the threads and spoiling the design.

Thus every person has at his command a terrestrial and a celestial life. To the great majority entangled in the meshes of this world of illusions, these illusions appear to be the reality and the celestial life merely a dream : but there are others in whom the interior life has awakened, and who find the celestial life the real one, and this earthly life merely a dream or a nightmare. This fact of a double existence has been recognised by every sage and saint and is known to every one in possession of the divine knowledge of self. It is referred to in many places in the *Bhagavad Gita* and in the Bible. It is that double life of the initiated, to which the apostle refers, when he says : " We live upon the earth, but our consciousness is in heaven ".

There may be those in whom the light has entirely swallowed up the darkness : those in whom there exists no more " body of sin ". They are the fully developed Adepts, and as such a one St. Paul presents himself in his letter to the *Romans*, chap. vii., vv. 5 and 6,* where he says : " When we were in the flesh, the motions of sins which were by the law, did work in our members, to bring forth fruit unto death : but now we are delivered from the law—that being dead, wherein we were held—that we should serve in newness of spirit and not in the oldness of the letter ".

Such sages and saints are the *Buddhas* and *Arhats* and the " Masters of Wisdom " with whom H. P. B. claimed to have become acquainted, and with whom everyone may become acquainted, if he outgrows his own narrow little self and rises up to their plane. The circumstance that modern society does not know anything about the existence of holy persons and that modern science has not yet discovered any saints, does not invalidate the theory that there are human beings in whom the germ of Divinity contained in every person has become so much unfolded, that a higher realm of spiritual knowledge, unattainable by those who cling only to earthly things, has become revealed to them, and that the souls of such persons, having become self-conscious in the light of the Spirit, are in possession of extraordinary faculties. Of such regenerated ones the Bible states that they cannot sin, because *they are born of God.* (1 *John* iii. 9.) And in 1 *Peter* i. 33, we read that such souls having been purified in obeying the truth through the *spirit of unfeigned love*, are " born again, not of corruptible seed, but of incorruptible, by the *Word of God* " acting in them.

H. P. B. never made any claims of wanting her personality to be regarded as a god, saint or adept, and in a letter to the author of these notes she expressly repudiates such claims, saying that she is travelling on the Path, but has not yet attained the goal. There was still a merely human nature even in H. P. B.; she could still rejoice with the joyful, and sympathise with the sorrowing, and this part of H. P. B.'s nature was

---

* The Bible quotations contained in this article are not intended to imply that my views are based upon speculations on the sayings of the Bible : but are merely added as corroborative evidence for those who attribute any importance to them.

made the continual object of criticism by the " psychic researcher ", who knowing nothing about divinity in humanity, saw in her only his own animal image reflected. By such critics every nebulous spot in her nature was investigated and magnified by means of their own morbid imagination ; but the sunny side of her nature they did not perceive, because there was no light in themselves.

The sum and substance of what they discovered, if shorn of what their own fancy added to it, was that H. P. B. was kind and generous even to a fault : that she was impulsive and energetic and sometimes allowed herself to be carried into extremes by her noble impulses. They found that she smoked cigarettes, that she spoke her thoughts without much ceremony, and absolutely refused to be like these smooth-faced, sly and hypocritical saints, going about in continual disguise and being looked upon by the world as the pillars of church and state ; while behind their sanctimoniousness is hidden nothing but rottenness and conceit. The screech owls of scientific sophistry that came to interview the eagle of the Himalayas found that they could not follow its flight to mountain summits that were entirely beyond the range of their limited vision, and as they could not clip its wings, their envy became aroused and they hooted and chattered, hurling calumnies at the royal bird. In many instances these calumniators overdid their work, and the extraordinary vituperance of their vilifications contains sufficient evidence of the character of the spirit that inspired such writings, so as to render any refutation quite unnecessary.

Some such writers charged her with having committed immoral practices, and all such stories, as soon as they were invented, found their way into print and were always readily taken up and circulated by those intrepid newspaper-writers who are ever on the alert, anxious to increase the circulation of their papers, by giving to their readers something spicy and sensational. Such stories were often exquisitely absurd and caused no little hilarity among those who were acquainted with the facts. Thus I remember that while I was in India, a story made its round through some English and American papers, saying that a row had occurred among the Theosophists at Adyar, because H. P. B. had become jealous of Col. Olcott, on account of Madame Coulomb, and that Mr. Coulomb had in his rage refused to furnish any more funds to carry on the business of the Theosophical Society. Those who are acquainted with the persons referred to, and know that the Coulombs were penniless and were suffered to remain at Adyar for charity's sake, will appreciate the roar with which this " news " was received by the " Chelas ".

There would have been no end of writing and wasting of time, if all the slanders about H. P. B., that were circulated by the pious missionaries of Madras and elsewhere, had had to be refuted, especially as it is far easier to make a calumnious assertion, than to disprove it. Some of these calumnies may however have been made with the best of intentions ; for instance certain persons threw doubts upon H. P. B.'s veracity, for the same reason that prompted a certain African king to order the beheading of a European traveller : because the latter had told the king, that in certain parts of Europe and at certain seasons, the water of the rivers and lakes became so firm that one could walk upon it ; whereupon the king decided that such a liar should not be suffered to live.

I would have but little regard for the truth, if I were to attempt to claim that none of the accusations brought forth against H. P. B. had any foundation in facts ; but the principal cause that brought troubles without end upon her, was her entire want of judgment in regard to the manner in which worldly affairs must be conducted, a childlike trust that the world would look at things in the way they appeared to her ; an entire disregard as to what the public would say or think about her ; a desire to shield her followers from the consequences of stupidities committed by them, &c., &c. What H. P. B. wanted she thought, and what she thought she said, and what she said she acted, regardless of any consequences. In her, as in an innocent child, thoughts, words and acts were one and in harmony.

If we were to attempt to solve the mystery of the "Sphinx of the nineteenth century" and give a history about the true *Ego* of H. P. Blavatsky, we would first of all have to learn who is the individuality, the " new creature " * that was embodied in the form of H. P. B., and know something of its previous lives, so as to be able to understand what caused it to appear in a woman's form upon this earth. We would then have to accept the theory that the soul of the regenerated is capable of living and acting beyond the limits of the physical form which is its dwelling and instrument for outward manifestation, and that the spiritual soul of such a person may be in an ethereal astral form in some distant country—say in Tibet—while the physical body is still living and acting consciously and intelligently in Europe and America. But the world is not yet ripe enough to receive a serious history, containing facts which are still a *terra incognita* to Europe and science, and whose correspondencies are to be found only in the *Acta Sanctorum*, which now-a-days are regarded even by the church as being " legendary and fabulous ", or (to express it less politely) as being a tissue of lies. Such a history would require readers acquainted with the doctrines of *Reincarnation* and *Karma* ; readers that had themselves conquered their own nature, and by their own experience had been enabled to realise what it means to be in the world but not of it.

But although the Bible says : that "except a man be born again he cannot see the kingdom of God " (*John* iii. 3), nevertheless the terms "rebirth " and " regeneration " have become words without any meaning to the modern religionist, and absurdities to the scientist. The religious visionary flatters himself with believing that he is already regenerated and has attained immortality. He does not know that regeneration in

---

* *Gal.* vi. 15.

the spirit is accompanied with an opening of the spiritual senses, and that his "regeneration" cannot have taken place as long as he is blind to the light of the truth and deaf to the "voice of the silence". "Re-generation" now-a-days is a word without meaning to the man of the world, and to the churchman it means at best a change of belief and an improvement of morals. The modern "Christian" has no understanding for such passages of his Bible, as the following: "My little children, of whom I travail in birth again *until Christ be formed in you*". (*Galat*. iv. 19.) "In Christ Jesus neither circumcision availeth anything, nor uncircumcision, but *a new creature*." (*Galat*. vi. 15.) Etc., etc. They do not believe what their teacher says of his true followers, that the regenerated ones, those in whom "the Son of God has come to the measure of the stature of the fulness of Christ" (*Ephes*. iv. 13) will do the same wonderful things that he performed himself. They do not believe that no one can possibly be in possession of conscious immortality, unless the "new creature" has been born in him, and they flatter themselves in presuming that their spirit is already immortal. But the Spirit immortality of the Spirit of God will not render their souls immortal, if their souls refuse to be fructified by that Spirit of God and to bring forth the divine child.

Let such "Christians" reflect about the meaning of the words of the Bible, where it says: "Marvel not that I said unto thee, Ye must be born again. That which is born of the flesh is flesh, and that which is born of the Spirit is Spirit. Except a man be born of water and of the Spirit, he cannot enter into the kingdom of God." (*John* iii., 5.) Little will it serve the sanctimonious to believe that their spirit is immortal, as long as they have no spirit which they can properly call their own; because their soul contains no divine love or spirit, and therefore cannot generate the "new creature" which can claim immortality in the Christ. This union of the mortal soul with the immortal Spirit is the end and object of all Occultism and Theosophy. It was this regeneration that H.P.B. taught; for "*spiritual regeneration*" *and* "*initiation*" *are synonymous terms.*

But a doctrine which does not flatter men's vanity by making men believe that they are already immortal, owing to the merits of a person that lived in the past, but claims that immortality is a boon, gained only by heroic efforts in battling with the lower elements in our nature, which prevent the action of divine grace within ourselves, is not welcomed by those who prefer to run after money and pleasures and expect to ride after death into heaven upon the back of another man; and therefore the history of a regenerated soul would be believed or understood only by few. Much easier would it be to clothe such a history in the fictitious form of a novel, that makes no claims for belief and in which everyone may believe as much as he is capable of understanding and put away the rest.*

---

* In the "Talking Image of Urur" such facts have been portrayed. There the "Master of the Image" represents the true *Ego*, the regenerated soul, while the Image itself is merely the elementary body, the personality, through which the true *Ego* acts.

To understand the true mystery that surrounded H. P. B., it will first be necessary to understand the mystery called "Man": for the Initiate, compared with the vulgar, is like a bird in comparison with an egg. The bird knows of eggs and their history, but the eggs know nothing of the existence of birds. To solve the great mystery called man, mankind will have to crawl out of the "philosophical egg" and, by becoming free, attain the noble self-knowledge of Divinity in Humanity; but at the present time there seem to be few, even among the so-called "Theosophists", having the faintest conception of what "divine self-knowledge" means.

Owing to the universal misconception existing in regard to the true nature of man and the ignoring of all that is divine in that nature, H. P. B. has been universally misunderstood and misrepresented. After a long and patient observation, a conviction which I persistently refused to accept forced itself upon me, namely, that in this respect far more harm has been done by H. P. B.'s over-zealous friends and admirers, than by her enemies. H. P. B. never asked to be deified, and denied the possession of miraculous powers; but there were many of her followers carrying on a fetish worship with her person, making the wildest and most extravagant statements on her behalf, which on investigation were found to be worthless, and thus only brought discredit upon her and her Society, while, with very few exceptions, these enthusiastic friends were the first ones to desert her or become her enemies, when the illusions, which they themselves had created, exploded.

According to the stories, generated, believed and circulated by such admirers, H. P. B. was continually attended by spirits; invisible "Masters from Tibet" danced attendance on her; they either *verbatim* dictated her writings to her or "precipitated" her manuscripts while she was taking her nap.* Gnomes, sylphs, undines and salamanders were at all times at her command, carrying her letters and superintending the kitchen. There was nothing going on in any part of the world which—according to their statements—H. P. B. did not know: but it was only too evident to outsiders, that H. P. B. did not know everything, and that even in her greatest troubles the fairy post did not work; but that for receiving information she, like other mortals, had to depend upon terrestrial mails and telegraphs. The fact is, that at the bottom of all such statements there was a certain amount of truth, but the facts were exaggerated beyond all limits by her over-enthusiastic friends.

H. P. B., according to her own confession, was not a learned woman. She was not even clever. On the contrary, all the great things she did were performed by her and some of her associates in the most bungling possible manner, which often spoiled the good result, and in calling her

---

* After the above was written, LUCIFER of May 15th comes to my hands, where I find this statement singularly corroborated by herself on page 243.

" the greatest impostor of the age" the agent of the *Soc. Psych. Res.*, who presented her with that title, merely certified to his own incapacity to judge about character, for H. P. B.—as all who were acquainted with her will testify—was never capable of disguising herself, and any imposture, great or little, which she could have attempted, would have immediately been found out, even by a child. H. P. B. was neither clever nor " smart ", but she was in possession of that in which most of her critics are sadly deficient, namely, *soul-knowledge*, a department of " science " not yet discovered by modern scientists and would-be philosophers. The soul that lived in her was a great soul, a *Mahatma* (from *Maha*, great, and *Atma*, soul). This great soul, and not the dress which H. P. B. used to wear, should be the object of our investigation, not for the purpose of gratifying scientific curiosity—but for profiting by the example.

Now, it appears to me that I hear a thousand voices ask the question : What is the knowledge of the soul, and how can it be obtained ? Is there any other knowledge than that of the reasoning brain ? Can we know of any other thing than what we have been taught in our school, what we have read in books, or what we remember of having heard ? To this we would answer : Woe to the people that does not know by heart that which is good and beautiful. Woe to those who have no interior perception for justice and truth ; who cannot *feel* true love, hope and faith, and who have to study the encyclopædia to find out the meaning of the terms benevolence, charity, generosity, spirituality, virtue, etc., etc. All these things are not creations of the imagination, nor products of the physical body ; but spiritual living powers, endowing with their qualities the soul that is in possession of them. If these powers are permitted to grow and to become unfolded, then will their true nature become clear to the mind, but no amount of intellectual speculation will enable him who possesses them not, to realise what they are.

The study of these powers and the art of developing them by practice formed the science of the soul, which Madame Blavatsky taught. All the rest of her doctrines, regarding the constitution of man, the evolution of worlds, etc., etc., were merely accessories to facilitate self-knowledge ; to destroy bigotry and superstition, and by freeing the mind from prejudices, to give it a wider range of ennobling thought, and enable it to form a grander and higher conception of God, Nature and Man. What can such a study have to do with the ghost stories, psychic researchers, coffee pots, trapdoors, and other tomfooleries, that haunt the minds of those who seek in external things for tests of the existence of things which they ought to possess themselves, before they can truly deserve to be called men made in the image of God ? Verily those who became her enemies because she could not gratify their curiosity ought to be blamed themselves for their wilful rejection of divine truth.

The first thing necessary for the acquisition of soul knowledge is the *possession of a soul*, which means the power to feel. Among the opponents of H. P. B. very little of the soul element is to be found. They seem to exist entirely on the plane of the mind, that part of man which only reasons and speculates ; but which has no actual knowledge, and which the ancient writers compared with the cold moonshine, because there is nothing in it of the warm sunshine of love. The element of the soul is the will, and the divine will is universal love ; such as creates a paradise—not in the imagination, but in the hearts of those who are in possession of it. When the morning star of divine love arises within the soul, peace enters with it. Therefore it is not said, that the angels at the time when the Christ is born within the human heart sing : " Glory be to those who are well versed in science and sophistry " ; but they are said to sing : " Glory be to that God who is universal Love, and peace to all men who are of good (*i.e.* divine) will ".

A large amount of learning may be stuffed into a brain during one lifetime, and when death arrives, all this now worthless rubbish, having no value whatever in the realm of eternity, will be abandoned, but the unfoldment of the divine lotus-flower of the soul in the sunshine of divine love may require many successive incarnations. With the first ray of that love, assimilated by the soul and rendering it conscious of its own higher nature and destiny, "Chelaship " descends upon the pilgrim on the road that leads to initiation and immortality. As the fire of love is kindled within the heart, the light therefore arises and illuminates the mind, and produces certain changes even in the physical form. (*Ephes.* iv. 16.) Without this divine love all learning is useless, all efforts vain : for God is Himself Love (1 *John* iv. 8.), and there can be no unification or atonement with God if Love is rejected. (1 *Corinth.* xiii. 2.) He who finds Love finds spiritual Life (*Proverbs* viii. 35), but he who rejects love rejects light and chooses darkness and death. Man has been called a " mixed being ", because he is not wholly material, but also spiritual in his nature. In him (as Jacob Böhme says) is the battleground of three kingdoms : the kingdom of light, the kingdom of darkness, and the realm of nature. " Forever the daylight shines into the darkness, and the darkness comprehendeth it not " ; but when the darkness is swallowed up by the light and the Spirit in man awakens to his divine self-consciousness, then will arise in man a new set of interior faculties, a new range of spiritual perceptions and powers, and the memory that belongs to the internal re-incarnated *Ego* will come within the grasp of the terrestrial outward mind. These teachings, which are incomprehensible to the many, because they deal with things that are beyond the range of their experience, are of the highest importance for the encouragement of the few who desire to follow the path travelled by that soul which was incarnated in the body of H. P. Blavatsky, and we should therefore, instead of wasting our time with the investigation of such trivialities as belonged to her personality (for instance, the omission of a quotation-mark), attempt to study her interior life and follow her soul on its upward flight towards the throne of Divine Wisdom.

FRANZ HARTMANN, M.D.

Reminiscences of Madame Blavatsky.

IT was in December, 1879, that I had the pleasure of first seeing Madame Blavatsky, when she was on a visit to Mr. and Mrs. Sinnett, and I am glad to say that the friendship which ensued lasted without diminution until the day of her death. I had, while in England in 1878, investigated the phenomena of spiritualism, and a lady spiritualist whom I had met while investigating, suggested, when writing to me in India, that I should make Madame's acquaintance if opportunity offered. Curiosity, and a desire to meet Mr. and Mrs. Sinnett—the former of whom I had corresponded with as Editor of the *Pioneer*—induced me to take a long journey of about thirty hours to Allahabad for this purpose ; and no journey in my life has ever repaid me so well, or been the source of so much and such permanent satisfaction. So many Theosophists have written eulogies on our late friend and teacher—H.P.B., as she preferred being called—that I feel it will be preferable for me to confine myself to a short account of my impressions of her character and of some of the incidents which occurred during this brief visit to Allahabad, and afterwards when we again met at Simla.

Eastern philosophy has now, very rightly, taken the chief place in connection with the Theosophical Society, and her name will be handed down to posterity rather as the exponent of these doctrines, than as a wonder worker ; but at the time of which I am writing it was the phenomena which were associated with her name that attracted us to her. But it must be acknowledged that she always deprecated this craving for wonders, and spoke of such phenomena as "psychological tricks". Still our wish, and perhaps a little interest she herself had in proving her powers, induced her to show us some of these "psychological tricks", even while assuring us they were of no real value in comparison with the teaching which lay at the back of them. Mr. Sinnett's book, "The Occult World", gives so full an account of our early experiences, that I do not propose to go into any detail, but I feel that it is only due to her memory to say, in the face of the abuse which has been showered upon her both in life and after death, that I never saw anything, or have heard anything, which has led me for a moment to doubt the reality of the phenomena which occurred in her presence. And I also can say with perfect frankness, that although she was the most intellectual woman I have ever known, she was, I consider, so constituted that in her case systematic deceit was impossible. She had neither the cunning nor the self-control needful for plotting and conceal-ment ; and she lived so openly among her friends that the many falsehoods about her are absurd to those who have lived in the same house with her. She had the kindest of hearts, the most generous of dispositions, and with-out contending that she was perfect, she was one of those persons who are loved and respected most by those who know them most intimately. And you cannot pay anyone a greater compliment than this, I think. Her very failings, some of them, arose from a too open and generous nature, a too great readiness to accept every one who came to her and trust them. To myself and others it sometimes appeared strange that she seemed to have so little discernment of character ; but in some cases at least, it was a hope of doing good which probably induced her to tolerate and even appear friendly to those who afterwards turned against her and tried to injure her. How keenly she felt the shameful attacks upon her character we who knew her well, realized and regretted ; and I often tried to reason her into a feeling of indifference for the opinions of those who knew nothing of her except what they gathered from garbled and prejudiced accounts in news-papers. But although she personally felt these slanders, a large part of her suffering arose from a fear that the Cause which she had at heart, and for which she worked as I have never seen anyone else work in any other cause, would be injured by the calumnies against her. I always felt astonished at the untiring energy which she displayed ; even when ill she would still struggle to her writing-table and go on working. It fills one with contempt and anger to think that even when she was beyond the reach of slander some of the papers degraded their pages with abuse, and republished the falsehoods which have found credulous audience among a class who pride themselves on their incredulity.

I have, I find, left myself but little space for saying anything about the many interesting occurrences during our early intimacy, and perhaps on second thought a repetition of these is unnecessary, as they can be read elsewhere to better purpose. Still to show that I had ample opportunities for knowing her well, I will mention that during both her visits to Simla I saw her almost daily, in fact I was in the same house for three months, in and out of her room at any and all times of the day. She was always affectionate towards me, and I had a real affection for her, and shall always, as hitherto, defend her before the world. And we who know what a wonderful woman she was, and how interesting and profound is the philosophy which she has brought prominently forward, know also that a day will come when the world will acknowledge her greatness, and will realize that we who defend and reverence her memory are not such foolish and gullible people, as the conceited and usually ignorant public of to-day assume.

ALICE GORDON, F.T.S.

Madame Blabatsky and her Work.

IT was in April, 1884, that I first met Madame Blavatsky, and it was on the 26th of March, 1891, that I saw her for the last time, shortly before her death.

I well remember her arrival from Paris and her unexpected appearance at a meeting of the London Lodge of the Theosophical Society, which was being held at Lincoln's Inn. The impression made upon myself and others by her remarkable personality has never faded from my memory.

At that first meeting I recognised that I had met one whose influence on my life would be ineffaceable by time, and that having touched the very root and core of the inner nature that influence could never be set aside or ignored.

The few months of the summer of 1884 which she passed in our house in Elgin Crescent were marked by events of a curious and exceptional character, all alike bearing witness to the fact that the personality called Madame Blavatsky was different in most characteristics from those around, and crowds of visitors of all classes testified to the interest she evoked.

It was her custom while with us to devote the earlier part of the day to writing; she usually began at seven o'clock, but often earlier, and it was very rarely indeed that when I went into her room at about eight o'clock in the morning I did not find her already at her desk, at which she continued with a slight interval for lunch till about three or four o'clock in the afternoon. Then it was that the reception time began, and from early afternoon to late evening, one constant succession of visitors arrived. The old lady sitting in her armchair in the small drawing-room, which was barely large enough for the influx of guests, would be the centre of an enquiring circle. Many, of course, drawn by the fame of her great powers, merely came from curiosity. In those days the Psychical Research Society had not issued its famous report, and some of its members were often present, seeking the signs and wonders they so much desired to behold.

One afternoon a small party had assembled in the back drawing-room and among them some prominent members of the S.P.R. Madame Blavatsky was earnestly solicited to produce some phenomena. She laughingly answered, as she so often did to similar requests, " What do you want with phenomena? they are but psychological tricks and of little value to earnest students". However, she at length consented to try if she could do anything, and sitting among the others round the large table, she joined in conversation, and talk flowed on for a short time in the easy way it always did when she was surrounded with intellectual minds. In a very little while a strikingly sweet and crystal-like sound known as the astral bell made itself heard, and was repeated several times, to the great delight and pleasure of those who had never heard it before. The gentlemen present belonging to the S.P.R. professed themselves more than satisfied, remarking more than once that there could be no doubt as to the genuineness of that phenomenon. I might multiply instance after instance of phenomena, but knowing the value that Madame Blavatsky herself put upon these things, it would be but a poor tribute to her memory to put that forward which is but the least part of her work. But the Psychic Society Researchers and phenomena hunters, and those who only came to see and wonder, were but one portion of the great crowd. Many earnest minds engaged in scientific or philosophic study would come again and again, attracted by the power of an intellect that showed its vast strength in the way in which she dealt with the many subjects put before her.

Grave professors from Cambridge came and spent an occasional afternoon in her company, and I can see before me now the bulky form in the loose robe in the big armchair, with the tobacco basket by her side, answering deep and learned questions on theories of cosmogony and the laws governing matter, while twisting the little cigarettes which she constantly smoked herself and gave to her guests. To those friends who were in constant and unrestrained intercourse with her, other sides of her character were observable. She had an almost childish dependence upon others, alternating with great impatience of control, and her utter disregard of ordinary conventionality rendered life in a civilised community a burden to herself, and a continual trial to her friends in the endeavour to keep her from outraging the *convenances* of society. I believe her utter abhorrence of society shams often caused her to emphasize and delight in a certain bluntness of speech and rudeness of action that was sometimes perplexing even to her best friends. With all this she was easily moved by distress or pain in others, and was very kind to any children she came across. I remember one incident showing this aspect of her many-sided nature : she was at the Zoological Gardens in a bath-chair, when the little child of a friend fell just before her, against the wheel ; in her eagerness to assist the child she almost threw herself out of the chair, difficult as she alway found it to move, and was not satisfied till assured there was not much harm done. Little touches like this shew plainly that in spite of her roughness of speech and manner, and the disregard she often had for the feelings of others, she had yet much sympathy towards the weak and suffering.

When she first came to us she brought with her her Indian servant (Babula), and it was an essential feature of the afternoon to see him in his native dress bring in the Russian Samovar, and hand round the cups of tea to those present ; altogether the 77, Elgin Crescent of those days differed widely from what it ever was before or ever will be again.

The whole party had received an invitation from Mr. and Mrs. Gebhard, of Elberfield, to spend the month of August at their house ; accordingly, on the 16th of that month Madame Blavatsky, accompanied by Mr. M. Chatterji and several Theosophists, ourselves among the number, went to Germany.   I remember well most of the incidents of that journey, the kind care of our host Mr. Gebhard, who took every precaution to render it as easy as possible to Madame Blavatsky, the pleasant and lively conversation among us all in the train, the notice we attracted at some of the stations in Germany, where we stopped and where probably no such type as Mr. Chatterji had ever been seen before, and many other details which, although interesting to those who were present, are of too personal a nature to be in place in this slight notice.   It was while staying with these kind friends that the explosion of the Coulomb affair took place.   The particulars of all that occurred at that time are well known, and it is quite unnecessary for me to touch on them, the more so as we had left Madame at Elberfeld and had returned to London before we heard of it.

It was in the end of September that Madame Blavatsky again came to us for a short time before going to Mr. and Mrs. Oakley, previous to their all leaving for India.   She was very depressed and unwell, almost worn out with the trouble that she had gone through.   In a letter that she wrote me at that time, just before leaving Elberfeld, she says : " I have resigned my corresponding secretaryship in the Society ; I have disconnected myself with it publicly ; for I think that so long as I am in and at the head of the Society I will be the target shot at and that the Society will be affected by it "—and she goes on to say, " My heart—if I have any left—is broken by this step.   But I had to sacrifice myself to the good of the Society. The *Cause* before persons and personalities."

This devotion to the *Cause* was the keynote of her life, from which she never departed.   She failed many times in the discrimination of what was or the good of the cause, as she did in this instance, when she contemplated disconnecting herself from her official position, but it is impossible to ignore the fact that, whether rightly or wrongly carried out, her motive for action was always the same devotion to the Cause and her Teachers. She was fortunately prevented from carrying out her intention, over-ruled by the wiser judgment of others who, being a little more distant from the fray, could view the situation more calmly.

There are many occasions that I remember during her stay with us of conversations or rather monologues on her side of a most interesting character.   It was my custom, one which she always encouraged, to go in to her the last thing at night and I would often remain until she was asleep.   At these times she would occasionally relate short stories, sometimes a kind of allegory and at other times what seemed to be incidents in a past life, either of herself or some other person, but so poetically and yet graphically related, that whether it was fact or fancy needed intuition to decide. Question she would not brook ; if I ever attempted to question she would be silent, or say, " I have said it ; you can make what you like of it ".

In November of that same year, many of us accompanied her to Liverpool, when she left for India with Mr. and Mrs. Oakley, and from that time, with the exception of a week in Würzburg and an occasional visit in London, my personal intercourse with Madame Blavatsky was over. Difficulties, trials and events of a more or less painful nature were constantly occurring during her stay with us, and yet I should be sorry not to have had this intimate association with one who, whatever her faults may have been, has certainly accomplished one of the greatest works of her time.

With respect to her work there is one aspect of it which I should wish to bring before the notice of all, whether Theosophists or not—a work which I think has hardly been sufficiently estimated and which nevertheless is of the utmost importance, whether viewed from the physical or spiritual standpoint. In our relations with the East we have hitherto only acted from the principle of give and take in self-interest. No one will deny the advantages derived on both sides from the presence of the English in India, wealth and prestige on the one, education and material development on the other. But a line of separation has been drawn between the two races, a line which has but been accentuated by the missionary in his vain endeavour to bring over the dark sons of the soil to the religion of the dominant race. The endeavour has signally failed, and yet it has perhaps more than anything else divided the East from the West. The Orientalist in his study of Eastern language, literature, and religion, has at different times attempted to pass the barrier, but his own pride of race and arrogance of knowledge have been a fatal obstacle in the way. The idea that it is only through Western interpretation that Eastern philosophy can be unravelled and that whatever that interpretation is unable to deal with is but the vain nonsense and babbling of children, is the rock against which most students of Oriental philosophy have fallen.

It has been the glorious work of Madame Blavatsky to entirely take a fresh departure. *Ex Oriente Lux* is henceforward the motto, and the light is to be found through Eastern sources, interpreted through Eastern teachers. The future of India is the future of England politically, materially, and spiritually ; and it is the drawing together of the East and the West in the bonds of spiritual philosophy, which I consider one of the most salient features for good in the work of the Theosophical Society. The marked advance in the knowledge we are gaining day by day of Indian philosophic history must be evident to all. A few years ago and there were scarcely any translations of Sanskrit philosophical works, and the knowledge of Sanskrit itself was limited to a few students here and there. The whole tendency of the teaching of Madame Blavatsky has been to awaken

India to a knowledge of its past spiritual life, and to bring that life to be better understood by the Western World. The evidences that mark the work accomplished in this direction are to be found in the various translations constantly being brought out of Sanskrit works, and the efforts of Europeans, both in and out of the Society, to seek that wisdom which has been so long forgotten in India although never completely lost. The close union of the East and the West, in the unfoldment on the one side, and on the other the acceptance of this spiritual wisdom, will go far to minimise the painful effects of that struggle which must inevitably take place as the Eastern races rise to a sense of their own power in the pursuit of material advantage.

Much more might be said on this subject, but this is not the place ; it is sufficient here to acknowledge gratefully that in this aspect, as well as others, Madame Blavatsky has been the leader in a work · which we who claim to have been her pupils would do well to endeavour to carry forward.

FRANCESCA ARUNDALE.

Seeing Little ; Perceiving Much.

ANY valuable tribute to the character of Madame Blavatsky can come only from those who knew her far better than I. Yet no one who knew her at all, can be without some incidents or impressions illustrating the many-sidedness of the most marvellous personage of the century. I well remember my first words with her in August, 1887. I remarked that I naturally felt some trepidation at being in the presence of one who could read every thought. She replied that such an act would be dishonest. I said that I should not exactly call it " dishonest", though it might be unkind or intrusive. She answered, No, that it would be dishonest ; that she had no more right to possess herself of another person's secrets without his consent than of his purse : and that she never used the power unless either the person himself requested it, or the circumstances were of a kind to make it imperative. As I never had any desire to see phenomena, though fully believing in her occult prerogative, no suggestion for such ever arose. Yet on two occasions, both for a benign purpose, she made evident her occult perception. One was a verbal reference, remote but significant, to a matter known to no person living but myself. I was at the moment so astounded that I said nothing, and the subject was never re-opened—a reticence I now regret, since unrestrained conference might have resulted in great benefit to me, as was surely her design. The other occurred in a tender and beautiful letter cautioning me against misjudgment and quoting a phrase I had used in writing to an American friend. As if to make certain to me that she spoke from occult knowledge, she added that I had used that phrase on the same day when happened an exceedingly trivial incident consequent on my stooping to pick up an article dropped to the floor. Now, dates showed that the phrase could not have been repeated to her in time for her letter to me, and, in fact, I have since ascertained that it was never repeated to any one ; the incident referred to was too insignificant for any person to transmit across the Atlantic ; and the few who knew of the incident did not know of the phrase. Both facts, as well as the concurrent date, must therefore have been seen by her in the Astral Light.

A stay of over three weeks in her household during March, 1889, brought me more closely in contact with Madame Blavatsky, and fits me to perceive how true are the certifications of her character by those who have been nearest to her. But apart from this, and as a matter of individual experience, there are two facts which, as bearing upon her worth, may be the contribution from one who knew her limitedly as I did.

The first is an enlarging conviction of her wisdom. On a number of occasions I have felt assured that her judgment was at fault, and that time would soon prove it. As to each of these, with one possible exception whereon I have not all the facts, time has proved her to have been right and me wrong. One naturally acquires confidence in a superior who is always thus vindicated at one's own expense.

The second is an ever-increasing affection for her. I had not seen her for over two years before her departure, and my expressed desire was that she should never add to her labours by writing to me. Yet I have been ever conscious of a growing personal attachment, not mere reverence or loyalty nor even homage, but affection. Little deeds of kindness, gentle messages, thoughtful signs that no friend, however unimportant, was forgotten by the great heart which contained so much and yet lost sight of nothing, helped to feed a devotion which would anyhow have matured. If I have to bless her for great, transcendent benefit which illuminates each day of life, I can also thank her for words and acts which cheer it. And so it comes about that one who was not of those nearest her, nor yet of those long working for the Cause, can rank with those to whom no contemporary name is so tender, honoured, hallowed, sacred.

ALEXANDER FULLERTON, F.T.S.

Madame Blavatsky at a Distance.

IT was in the Spring of 1885 that I first heard the name of H. P. Blavatsky and the word " Theosophy ". We were at luncheon, and my hostess began opening her mail. She tossed one pamphlet impatiently aside, with the remark :

" Why do they send me that ? I am not a Theosophist."

" What is a Theosophist ? " queried I.

" A follower of Madame Blavatsky's Eastern teachings."

" And, pray, who is this Madame Blavatsky ? "

With an exclamation at my ignorance—an ignorance caused by circumstances which had removed me from all touch with the world of thought—my friend handed the discarded pamphlet to me, saying :

" Read that, and you will know her."

Prophetic remark ! " *That* " was the Report of the Society of Psychic Research, and through it I did come to know her. Read with care, it left two distinct impressions upon my mind.

First. Its amazing weakness as a verdict. My people on both sides had been lawyers for generations. I was accustomed to hear testimony discussed. The circumstantial nature of the evidence ; its fragmentary character ; the insufficiency of testimony ; the inadequacy of proof ; the fact that a single witness, sent out for the *purpose* of discovering suspected fraud, and a witness whose account of his proceedings showed credulity and want of equipoise, all combined to fill me with surprise that any body of men should consent to issue matter so feeble as their deliberate judgment. The Report bore no evidence to my mind save that of an immense prejudice, a predetermination to arraign and condemn.

The second impression left upon me related to Madame Blavatsky herself. I saw trace of her immense activity, her intellectuality, her work, and her influence. Evidently here was a power, whether for good, or for evil. Either she was an adventuress far surpassing all the world had ever known, an original adventuress who slaved for intellectual progress and rule as others slave for nothing, not even for gold—or she was a martyr. I could see no mean between. The force of her character took hold upon my imagination, and caused desire to know what were the teachings for which this woman braved—not alone obloquy, poverty, and persecution— but also the laughter of two continents, that laughter which is the deadliest weapon of the nineteenth century. So great impatience was engendered in me, so intense was my interest in the problem before me, that I went that same afternoon to hear a talk given by Mr. Arthur Gebhard in a private

salon, and all I heard convinced me, as by illumination, that the Theosophical teachings filled a life-long want of my nature; that they alone could
reconcile me to Life and to Death.

As these teachings shed their beneficent light upon my path, I
abandoned, so far as conscious thought was concerned, the fascinating
Blavatsky puzzle. The attempt to solve her character ended. I had
started upon an intellectual amusement; I had found a great Truth, found
a hint of the Holy Grail, and all else was forgotten in this. "It matters
not what Blavatsky is," I exclaimed; "Theosophy is the Truth. And
Truth is what avails; its adherents are nothing." It was only later on, as
the philosophy opened out before me, at once the lode-star and consolation
of my life, that I discovered within myself, quite by chance, as it were, a
profound, a passionate gratitude to that messenger who had dared all
things, given all things, endured all things to bring this priceless and
eternal gift to the Western world. She was my spiritual mother, my bene-
factor and my guide. In the light of this thought all lesser ones were
swallowed up. The need of understanding her character disappeared then,
to emerge later on. For the moment she was only, to me, that soul to
whom I owed the most. This indebtedness, no less than knowledge
of her untiring and enormous labours, seemed to spur me on to such
imitation as I could compass. For ever the idea that the only possible
return I could make to my benefactress was to give to others that bread of
life which she had given me, urged me to steadfast action. I seemed to
feel, across the intervening distance, the vast surge of her activity, and as
a thing to be sensed in all ways. It was as if what she had given was so
vital that it germinated within me; a life-impulse was imparted by her
soul to mine. I never had the same experience with any other person or
teaching. Only those who have passed through it can know the reality of
the "multiplication of energy" as possessed by certain great souls.
That which Keely has demonstrated to modern science—that the friction
of inter-etheric action, and the play of molecule against molecule, atom
against atom, *liberates* force instead of decreasing it, was here proven to
me, upon the psychic plane and from a distance, by the energic action of her
soul upon mine. It was tangible, verifiable; it had a pulse, ran through a
scale; alternated but never waned.

It was only at a later stage that the desire to understand Madame
Blavatsky returned. The immediate cause of this emergence was attack
made upon her. I felt a need to justify her, not alone to the world, but to
myself. That is, I believed in her. But I wanted to be able to put the
ground for that belief very clearly, to give reason (as well as intuition) for
it. I found myself amply able to do this, and for a very simple reason. It
became at once evident to me that the explanation of the personality of
Madame Blavatsky was to be found in the philosophy taught by her.
Message and messenger are one and the same thing in the laws of the

supra-natural, where, as Drummond puts it, cohesion is the law of laws. A person may *teach* a truth and yet may not *be* that truth, by virtue of living it. But he cannot impart a truth in its vitality, so that it fructifies— an energetic impulse of power—in other lives, unless he possesses that life-impulse by reason of his having become it. He cannot give what he has not. For example: after deducting, as unproven, a number of reports concerning H.P.B.—reports which time has abundantly disproven—I found that those hints of magnetico-etheric laws given by the Eastern school, would explain many of her words or ways, as endeavours to set up, alter, contract or expand given vibrations in the nerve-aura, or in the ether, both of which are dynamic agents of vast power when acted upon by certain sound-combinations known to the Adept. It was not, for instance, the philological meaning of the word she spoke which she intended to take effect upon the hearer, but its tone, or its sound, or its vibratory ratio, which set up effects upon the inner planes and met conditions therein existing which she alone could see and use to helpful ends. She always acted from the plane of the Real, and we had only physical senses where-with to gauge her spiritual action ; hence our failure. The fact that soul is independent of body, and may absent itself from the body, leaving only a residuum of force and reflected consciousness to run the body, accounted for other peculiarities ; and so on through the list. Nowhere could I find incongruity when I studied her from the stand-point of the inner and less unreal planes, and when I could not follow her mighty nature, I could still discern that, being what it was, it could only exist by virtue of going with the Law and not against it. When, in addition, I allowed for my own ignorance of Law and of those sub-rays called nature's laws or forces, the problem was answered. The fact of her existence thus became the most powerful factor of mine. Where I did well, she inspired me ; she, and what she gave forth. Where I did ill was where I departed from the philosophy and from her example.

I never met her, I never looked into her eyes. Words cannot picture regret. But after a time she wrote to me, of her own precedent and motion, as one who responds from afar to the longing of a friend. Prompt to reply if I asked help for another, silent only to the personal call ; full of pity and anguish for the mistaken, the deserter, the suffering ; solicitous only for the Cause, the Work, so I found her always. Although she had a lion heart, it bled ; but it never broke. The subtle aroma of her courage spread over seas, invigorated and rejoiced every synchronous heart, set us to doing and to daring. Knowing thus her effect upon our lives, in its daily incentive to altruistic endeavour, truth and virtue, we can smile at all alien testimony. Only from kindred virtues do these virtues spring. She could never have strengthened us in these things if she had not been possessed of them in abundant measure.

To quote the words of one who lived in the house with her : " They may say what they please about her personality. I never knew a better one. It had the sturdiness and dignity of the druidic oak, and she was well expressed by the druidic motto: '*The Truth against the World*'." Although in the flesh she remained unknown to me, she alone of all the world's Leaders gave me Truth, taught me how to find it, and to hold it " against the world ". The soul that can work such a miracle at a distance is no minor ray; it is one of the great Solar Centres that die not, even though for a time we miscall it Helena Blavatsky.

J. CAMPBELL VER PLANCK.

———— ✺ ————

What She taught Us.

IF I were to write this short memoir simply as an imperfect expression of what H. P. B. was to me personally, and of the influence of her life and teachings upon my own life and aspirations, I should merely be adding one more testimony to that affection and reverence which she inspired in all who learnt to understand her in some degree. There were those who were attracted to her by the magnetism of her personal influence, by her extraordinary intellect, by her conversational powers, and even by her militant unconventionality. But I was not one of these. It was her message that attracted me; it was as a teacher that I learnt to know and love her. Apart from her teachings I might have looked upon H. P. B. as an interesting and unique character, but I do not think I should have been attracted to her, had not her message spoken at once right home to my heart. It was through that message that I came to know H. P. B., not as a mere personal friend, but as something infinitely more.

Let me dwell therefore upon H. P. B. as a teacher, let me endeavour to express what it was that she set before me, and before so many others, the acceptance of which united us by ties which death cannot sever.

First, and above all else, she shewed us the *purpose of life*.

And when I say this I mean much more than might be commonly understood by this phrase. I mean much more than that she gave us an interest and a motive in this present life, and a belief or faith with regard to the next. Those who have learnt the lesson of the illusory nature of that which most men call *life*, whether here or hereafter, need to draw their inspiration from a deeper source than is available in the external world of forms. But to the born Mystic there is often a long period of waiting and seeking before that source is found. Many years are spent in testing and rejecting first one system, then another, until it seems perchance as if life could be naught but a hopeless problem. And perhaps just when all seemed darkest and most hopeless, when it even appeared best to abandon the quest, to take up the position, " we do not know, and we cannot know ", just then it has been that the light has dawned, the teacher has been sent, the word has been spoken, which has recalled the lost memory of that hidden source of truth for which we have been seeking ; and we have taken up once more, at the point at which we dropped it in a previous life-time, that great task which we have set ourselves to accomplish.

And thus she did something more than teach us a new system of philosophy. She drew together the threads of our life, those threads which run back into the past, and forward into the future, but which we had been unable to trace, and showed us the pattern we had been weaving, and the purpose of our work.

She taught us *Theosophy*—not as a mere form of doctrine, not as a religion, or a philosophy, or a creed, or a working hypothesis, but as *a living power in our lives*.

It is inevitable that the term *Theosophy* should come to be associated with a certain set of doctrines. In order that the message may be given to the world it must be presented in a definite and systematic form. But in doing this it becomes *exoteric*, and nothing that is *exoteric* can be permanent, for it belongs to the world of form. She led us to look beneath the surface, behind the form ; to make the *principle* the real motive power of our life and conduct. To her the term *Theosophy* meant something infinitely more than could be set before the world in any *Key to Theosophy*, or *Secret Doctrine*. The nearest approach to it in any of her published works is in *The Voice of the Silence;* yet even that conveys but imperfectly what she would— had the world been able to receive it—have taught and included in the term *Theosophy*.

The keynote of her teachings, the keynote of her life, was—*Self-sacrifice*.

" But stay, Disciple . . . Yet one word. Canst thou destroy divine COMPASSION ? Compassion is no attribute. It is the LAW of LAWS— —eternal Harmony, Alaya's SELF ; a shoreless universal essence, the light of everlasting Right, and fitness of all things, the law of love eternal . . . Now bend thy head and listen well, O Bôdhisattva—Compassion speaks and saith : ' Can there be bliss when all that lives must suffer ? Shalt thou be saved and hear the whole world cry ? ' "

And thus though doctrinal Theosophy speaks of *Devachan* and *Nirvana :* of rest for the weary storm-tossed pilgrim of life ; of a final goal of bliss past all thought and conceiving ; yet, to those who are able to receive it, it says that there is something higher and nobler still, that though thrice great is he who has " crossed and won the Aryahata Path ", he is greater still, who having won the prize can put it aside, and "remain unselfish till the endless end ".

And so H. P. B. often pointed out to us those men and women who were true Theosophists, though they stood outside of the Theosophical movement, and even appeared antagonistic to it. Already in the world a

Theosophist has come to mean someone who believes in Re-incarnation and Karma, or some other distinctive doctrine. But the term was never so limited in its application by the great founder of the Theosophical Society. She taught these doctrines in order that men might dissociate themselves from *all forms* of doctrine, and reach " Alaya's Self ". There is no older doctrine than this of Divine Compassion, of Universal Brotherhood. It is the essence of all the teachings of all the Buddhas and Christs the world has ever known. It is above all doctrines, all creeds, all formulas; it is the essence of all religion. Yet men ever miss it, miss the one principle which alone can save the world, and take refuge instead in the selfish desires of their lower nature.

Individualism is the keynote of modern civilization; competition and survival of the fittest, the practical basis of our morality. Our modern philosophers and scientific teachers do all that is possible to reduce man to the level of an animal, to show his parentage, his ancestry and his genius as belonging to the brute creation, and conditioned by brutal laws of blind force and dead matter. What wonder then that one who believed so ardently in the divine nature of man, in the divine law of love, should oppose with scornful contempt the teachings of both religion and science which thus degrade humanity.

And she paid the inevitable penalty. Misunderstood, slandered, and vilified to the last degree, she lived a hero's life, and died a martyr's death. Only those who were her intimate friends knew how she suffered, mentally and bodily. The man who dies with his face to the foe, fighting to the last though covered with wounds, is accounted a hero. But in the heat of battle there is oblivion of pain, there is a superhuman strength of madness and frenzy. How much more should she be accounted a hero who could hold on to life, and work as no other woman has worked, through years of physical and mental torture.

Some few years ago she was at death's door. Humanly speaking, she ought to have died then. She was given up by the doctors; she herself knew she was dying, and rejoiced greatly. But the Master came to her, showed her the work that must still be done, and gave her her choice—the bliss of dying or the cross of living.

She chose the cross. And thus not merely did she teach us the meaning of Theosophy by precept, but also by example. She was herself the greatest of the Theosophists, not merely because she founded the movement, and restored to the world the treasures of ancient wisdom, but because she herself had made the " *Great Renunciation* ".

WILLIAM KINGSLAND, F.T.S.

From India.

[BABULA, H. P. B.'s Hindu servant, writing from Adyar, sends a leader that appeared in the *Indian Mirror* of May 13th. "Humanity", he says, "has sustained an irreparable loss from her sudden death. With tears in my eyes I wrote this brief note." We print the leader among these memorial articles as a testimony from the East that she loved so well.]

"Gone is the glory from the grass,
And splendour from the flower!"

HELIONA PETROVNA BLAVATSKY has ceased to exist on this earthly plane. She is gone from among us. Madame Blavatsky's death is a blow to all the world. She was not of this nation or that. The wide earth was her home, and all mankind were her brothers, and these brothers are now plunged in mourning for the loss of a priceless sister. For ourselves, dazed as we are with blinding grief, it is all impossible for us to realise the enormity of this loss. Our affection for Madame Blavatsky was so personal, we were so longing to see her in flesh once more in India, and to press her hallowed hand, that now that this desire has been cruelly crushed by death, a stupor has crept over all our senses, and we are writing as if it were mechanically. We recall the features of the dear lady, who is assuredly a saint now, her quick movements, the rapid flow of words, those light, glowing eyes, which saw through you and, at a glance, turned you inside out—anon we behold her, kind and gentle as a mother, and wise as a father, pouring faith, hope, and consolation into your ears, as you mention to her your doubts and your anxieties—there Madame Blavatsky, or H. P. B., as she loved to be called, and as loving friends always called her in affection, there H. P. B. stands before us now, all herself, free from disease, and, seems to whisper to us the larger faith, which animated her through life, that trust in the infinite purpose, which is both the *karma* and the destiny of the Divine Man!

Madame Blavatsky was decidedly the most remarkable person that this age has produced. The whole of her life was simply extraordinary. There is no existing human standard by which to judge her. She will always stand out alone. There was only one Madame Blavatsky, there never will be any other. It was always difficult to understand her at all points, she was often the greatest puzzle to her most intimate friends, and the mystery of her life is yet only partly revealed. But future generations will have come at a sufficient distance of time to free them from circumstantial prejudices, and to pronounce an accurate judgment on Madame Blavatsky's life and work, and we say confidently that before many years have gone by, she will be regarded as an Avatar, a holy incarnation, and divine honours will be paid to her memory.

The story of Madame Blavatsky's life appeared while she was yet alive, and has been read with wonder everywhere. There is no parallel to such a biography as Mr. Sinnett has related. It is a story of a wayward and fanciful child, slowly budding into womanhood, enjoying curious experiences, and astonishing and frightening in turns the inmates of a noble and fashionable Russian home. Then comes the marriage with General Blavatsky, whom the girl took for husband for very frolic, and ran away from immediately after without allowing him time or opportunity to enforce his conjugal rights. Then we follow the high-souled and eccentric woman in her wanderings in the East, obedient to the occult call, which she heard far back in her childhood. And the East has claimed her as its very own ever since. But her bones have not been laid in the East. Our readers will remember that such a hope had been expressed by us only a few days ago, but, at that time, we had no fears that her death would occur so soon. In fact, we were preparing to invite her back, and entreat her to pass her declining years in India. For India, or rather Tibet, was the promised land for Madame Blavatsky. It was there that she acquired her extraordinary learning and her wonderful knowledge of the world-old religions and philosophies of the East, and ever humbly and gratefully she professed herself to be the slave and the worldly instrument of the Masters, who received, taught and protected her. But for the Masters, she would have died before long, for during her world-wide wanderings she had contracted germs of many and complicated diseases. Before her final departure from India, her life had been given up, and it was a veritable marvel to her physicians that she did pull through. But at that time, she had not yet completed her life-work. The message of the Masters had not yet been fully delivered. It was subsequently given to the world in that monumental work, *The Secret Doctrine*.

Madame Blavatsky may be literally said to have lived and died for India. The Theosophical Society was founded expressly for disseminating the religious and philosophic truths of Vedanta and Buddhism among the Western nations. But those truths were known very partially in this country itself. Madame Blavatsky was accordingly required to transfer her labours among us, and for several years she became a living sacrifice for the sake of the Hindus, who, however, turned away most ungratefully from her, when she most needed their support. But now they have been rightly punished. Their land is not made sacred, as English ground has been, by her tomb or cenotaph. And English Theosophists have been certainly much more faithful to her than we in India have been. Theirs is and will be the exceeding great reward. But shall we not endeavour to wipe away the reproach and the shame? It can only be by raising such a memorial to Heliona Petrovna Blavatsky's memory as shall show the strength and extent of our repentance, and our appreciation of all that she ever did for India.

"H.P.B.'s" Departure.

THERE are certain bereavements which one would prefer to bear in silence, since words are too poor to do them justice. Under such an one the members of the Theosophical Society, and I, especially, are now suffering. Our loss is too great for adequate expression. Ordinary friends and acquaintances may be replaced, even in time forgotten, but there is no one to replace Helena Petrovna, nor can she ever be forgotten. Others have certain of her gifts, none has them all. This generation has not seen her like, the next probably will not. Take her all in all, with her merits and demerits, her bright and her dark moods, her virtues and her foibles, she towers above her contemporaries as one of the most picturesque and striking personages in modern history. Her life, as I have known it these past seventeen years, as friend, colleague and collaborator, has been a tragedy, the tragedy of a martyr-philanthropist. Burning with zeal for the spiritual welfare and intellectual enfranchisement of humanity, moved by no selfish inspiration, giving herself freely and without price to her altruistic work, she has been hounded to her death-day, by the slanderer, the bigot and the Pharisee. These wretches are even unwilling that she should sleep in peace, and are now defiling her burial urn in the vain hope of besmirching her memory—as the Roman Catholics have those of Cagliostro and St. Germain, her predecessors—by their mendacious biographies. Their scheme will fail, because she has left behind her a multitude of witnesses ready to do justice to her character and show the purity of her motives. None more so than myself, for, since our first meeting in 1874, we have been intimate friends, imbued with a common purpose and, in fraternal sympathy, working on parallel lines towards a common goal. In temperament and abilities as dissimilar as any two persons could well be, and often disagreeing radically in details, we have yet been of one mind and heart as regards the work in hand and in our reverent allegiance to our Teachers and Masters, its planners and overlookers. We both knew them personally, she a hundred times more intimately than I, and this made the rupture of our relationship as unthinkable a question as the dissolution of the tie of uterine brotherhood. She was to me a sister in a peculiar sense, as though there had been no period of beginning to our alliance, but rather a psychical consanguinity which dated from anterior earth-lives. She was pre-eminently a double-selfed personality, one of them very antipathetic to me and some others. Her almost constant ill-health and the want of touch between herself and modern society made her irritable, unquiet and often—I thought—unjust.

But she was never commonplace. I loved her for the other, the higher self, which was also the most mysterious. One seeing us together would have said I had her fullest confidence, yet the fact is that, despite seventeen years of intimacy in daily work, she was an enigma to me to the end. Often I would think I knew her perfectly, and presently discover that there were deeper depths in her self-hood I had not sounded. I never could find out *who she was*, not as Helena Petrovna, daughter of the Hahns and Dolgoroukis, whose lineage was easy to trace, but as " H.P.B.," the mysterious individuality which wrote, and worked wonders. Her family had no idea whence she drew her exhaustless stream of curious erudition. I wrote and asked her respected aunt the question, soon after the writing of " Isis Unveiled " was begun, but she could afford no clue. Madame Fadeyef replied : " When I last saw her "—some five years previously—" she did not know, even in her dreams, the learned things you tell me she is now discussing ". I helped H.P.B. on that first of her wonderful works, " Isis," and saw written or edited every page of the MSS. and every galley of the proof-sheets. The production of that book, with its numberless quotations and its strange erudition, was quite miracle enough to satisfy me, once and for all, that she possessed psychical gifts of the highest order. But there was far more proof than even that. Often and often, when we two were working alone at our desks far into the night, she would illustrate her descriptions of occult powers in man and nature by impromptu experimental phenomena. Now that I look back to it, I can see that these phenomena were seemingly chosen with the specific design of educating me in psychical science, as the laboratory experiments of Tyndall, Faraday or Crookes are planned so as to lead the pupil *seriatim* through the curriculum of physics or chemistry. There were no Coulombs then above the mud, no third parties to befool, none waiting for jewelry presents, or Yoga powers, or special tips about the short cut to Nirvana : she merely wanted my literary help on her book ; and, to make me comprehend the occult laws involved in the moment's discussion, she experimentally proved the scientific ground she stood upon. More things were thus shown me that have never been written about, than all the wondrous works the public has read about her having done in the presence of other witnesses. Is it strange, then, that all the humbugging tales and reports by interested critics, about her trickery and charlatanry, failed to shake my knowledge of her real psychical powers ? And what wonder that I, who have been favoured beyond all others in the Theosophical Society with these valid proofs ; who was shown by her the realities of transcendental chemistry and physics, and the marvellous dynamic potencies of the human mind, will, and soul ; who was led by her into the delightful path of truth which I have ever since joyfully trodden ; and who was made personally to see, know, and talk with the Eastern Teachers—what wonder that I have loved her as a friend, prized her as a teacher, and evermore keep her memory sacred ? Living, I might quarrel with her, but dead, I must only bewail her irreparable loss, and redouble my exertions to push on our joint work.

This seems the proper moment to answer many questions as to what I think about the Patterson-Coulomb-Hodgson cabal against my dear friend. The hostile papers are rechauffing *ad nauseam* those funeral baked meats. Wherever I lectured in Australia there were muck-rakes to stir up the fæculent compost. I say, then, that I do not consider the charges proven. More than that nobody can go, unless he should have the gift of reading the innermost consciousness of the accusers and accused. On the very day when the charges against her were first published in the *Times*, she—then in London—wrote that paper an indignant denial. I have seen no proof since then to support the contrary. The alleged letters to Mme. Coulomb were never shown her or me; the Coulombs stand self-impeached as to honesty of character; Mr. Hodgson's report evinces his dense ignorance at the time of psychical and mediumistic laws and the indispensable rules of spiritualistic research, even of the commonest rules of legal evidence; the elaborate Nethercliff analysis of the Koot Hoomi and H.P.B. letters is a farce to the experienced psychologist, and moreover was completely nullified by the contradictory analysis made by the equally noted sworn expert of the Imperial High Court of Berlin; and H.P.B.'s life and labours distinctly give the lie to the injurious suppositions put forth against her. Finally, we have the convincing fact of her having exhibited weird psychical powers since her childhood, and especially while in New York, after the autumn of 1874, in the presence of many unimpeachable witnesses. I do not hesitate a moment, under the above circumstances, in accepting her simple denial in place of the most elaborate guessing and sophistical special pleading of her detractors. I may have been hypnotised, as alleged, but, if so, I do not know it.

Much has been made out of the fact that she did not go into Court to vindicate her character against the palpable libels of the Missionary and allied parties. For this *she is not to blame:* quite the contrary. But for my vehement protests she would have dragged the adversaries into the Madras Courts as soon as she got back from London, *via* Cairo, in 1884. A friend had offered her Rs. 10,000 to cover the expenses. It was then barely a fortnight before the time for the Annual Convention of our Society—December 27th, 1884—and I insisted upon her waiting until a Special Judicial Committee of the Convention should advise her as to her proper course. We were—I told her—the property of the Society, and bound to sink our private preferences and selves for the public good. She was stubborn to that degree, that I *had to threaten to quit my official position* before she would listen to reason. The Convention met, and the case was referred to a Committee composed of Hindu Judges and other legal gentlemen of high official and private standing. They unanimously reported against H.P.B.'s going to law; for one reason, because there was but the shadow of a chance of getting justice from a prejudiced Anglo-Indian jury, in any case involving questions of Eastern religious science *(Yoga)*, or the existence of (to process-servers) inaccessible Mahatmas ; and, for another, because neither a favorable nor unfavorable verdict would be likely to change the opinions of those respectively who knew, and did not know the truth about psychical powers *(Siddhis)*, and her possession of them ; while, finally, the most sacred feelings of Hindus and Buddhists were sure to be outraged by the ribald banter of counsel when cross-examining the witnesses as to matters of personal knowledge or belief. The Convention adopted unanimously the views of the Committee, and H.P.B. was forced to yield to the majority and nerve herself up to bear the consequences. The outrageous Salem Riot case, which was then fresh in the public memory, gave great weight to the Committee's decision in the present instance. Though restrained, H.P.B. was not convinced, and but for the constant opposition of her best friends, would have gone into Court at several later stages of the controversy, when the grossest personal insults were used as bait to entice her into the trap set by her enemies, whose bitterest spite has ever been against her personally. She chafed like a caged lioness, and thus aggravated her physical ailments, *viz.*, a form of Bright's disease, an affection of the heart, and a tendency towards apoplexy. The climate enfeebled her, and the worry was killing her so fast that her medical adviser at last gave me the following certificate :

" I hereby certify that Madame Blavatsky is quite unfit for the constant excitement and worry to which she is exposed in Madras. The condition of her heart renders perfect quiet and a suitable climate essential. I, therefore, recommend that she should at once proceed to Europe and remain in a temperate climate, in some quiet spot.

(Signed) MARY SCHARLIEB,
M.B. and B.Sc., *London*."

31-3-85.

Dr. Scharlieb privately warned me that H.P.B. was liable to drop down dead at any moment in one of her paroxysms of excitement. I lost no time after that—you may believe—in sending her away to Italy in the most unobtrusive way possible. Dr. Scharlieb's husband superintended her embarkation, providing the stretcher upon which she was carried, and arranging with the captain of the French steamer for hoisting her aboard from the small boat, in an invalid chair hung in slings. This was the pretended flight from Madras to escape being cited as a witness in a case then pending—for which calumny the Rev. Mr. Patterson, of the Scottish Mission, made himself responsible in print. Since that day our dear friend never saw India again in the body. From then until the day of her death she was under constant medical care, most of the time extremely ill and suffering. Twice or thrice I urged her to come out for at least one cold-weather season ; she was willing, but her physician, Dr. Mennell, positively refused consent, alleging that she would most probably die at sea. In January and February, 1885, she had been at death's door, and twice within a month I had been summoned back from Rangoon to receive her last wishes.

On the 21st March, 1885, she addressed the General Council, insisting upon their granting her permission to retire from office, saying: " My present illness is pronounced mortal by my medical attendants, and I am not promised even one certain year of life......I leave with you, one and all, and to every one of my friends and sympathizers, my loving farewell. *Should this be my last word, I would implore you all, as you have regard for the welfare of mankind and your own karma, to be true to the Society and not to permit it to be overthrown by the enemy.*

" Fraternally and ever yours, in life and death,

(Signed) H. P. BLAVATSKY."

And yet, despite her horrible physical state, she worked on at her desk twelve hours a day, year in and year out. The monuments of her literary industry between 1885 and 1891 are " The Secret Doctrine ", " The Key to Theosophy ", The Voice of the Silence ", " Gems from the East ", the several volumes of her new magazine *Lucifer*, her contributions in Russian and French to continental magazines, a great bulk of unpublished MSS. for Vol. III. of the " Secret Doctrine ", and her Esoteric Section, or private school of instruction in occult philosophy and science, which, at her death, numbered between one and two thousand pledged and enthusiastic pupils. Is this charlatanism, this tireless labour of brain and soul to collate and spread knowledge for the profit of others? If so, let us pray for the evolution of many charlatans. Does any unprejudiced person believe that one who could show such self-sacrifice and display such encyclopædic learning, would stoop to the petty and profitless trickery outlined in the insinuations and charges of her accusers? For pity's sake, let the dead lioness lie in peace, and seek a more ignoble carcase upon which to vomit.

It is amazing, the shallow falsehoods that have been—nay, are at this very hour of writing being—circulated against her. Among them, perhaps the wickedest are charges of immorality,* because the fact is—as a surgical certificate of an eminent German specialist proves—that she was physically incapable of indulging in such conduct, and of being a mother. This disposes of a number of vile stories to her prejudice. But nobody who had passed one day in her company could entertain the least suspicion of her feeling like other women in these matters—if there were ever a sexless being, it was she. Nor did she ever, in the years of our acquaintance, drink a glass of any kind of liquor. She smoked incessantly, no doubt, after her national Russian fashion, and she used strong language, and was eccentric to a degree, in most things of a conventional nature; but she was neither thief, harlot, drunkard, gambling-house keeper, nor any one of the other dozen criminal things she has been recklessly charged with being, by a set of scurvy writers not worthy of cleaning her shoes. Her day of

---

* Damnable calumnies which have been most widely circulated by conservative (!) papers.

vindication is not yet come, nor am I, long her most close friend, the fittest one to do her impartial justice. Yet it will come, and then the hand which pens the verdict of posterity will undoubtedly write her honoured name, not down among the poor charlatans who stake all upon the chance of profitless renown, but high up, beside that of Abou Ben Adhem, who loved his fellow men.

Upon receiving at Sydney by cable—and otherwise—the news of her sudden death, I cancelled my New Zealand and Tasmanian tours and took passage by the next steamer for Europe—on board which I am writing this with a heavy heart and stumbling pen. I have arranged by cable for a special meeting of the General Council at London, at which the future plans of the Society will be determined. While it will be impossible for us to replace H. P. B. by anyone this side the Himalayas, yet the work will go on as to its general lines without a moment's break. I have anticipated her death too many years to be discomfited and dis-heartened by it, now that the bolt has fallen. We had each our department of work—hers the mystical, mine the practical. In her line, she infinitely excelled me and every other of her colleagues. I have no claim at all to the title of metaphysician, nor to anything save a block of very humble knowledge. Even though not another page of mystical teaching should be given, there is quite enough to afford this generation key after key to unlock the closed portals of the hoary temple of truth. The thirsters after novelty may be downcast, but the real mystic will lack nothing which is essential.

Postscriptum.—Colombo, June 10th. Upon arrival, I get the full particulars of our direful catastrophe. H. P. B. breathed her last at 2.25 P.M. on Friday, the 8th May; sitting in her big arm-chair, her head supported by her dear friend Miss Laura Cooper, her hands held by Messrs. Wright and Old, members of her staff. Her devoted and unselfish physician, Dr. Z. Mennell, had left her but about an hour before, convinced that she would recover. There had been a sudden reaction, and, after an ineffectual struggle for breath, she passed out into the shadow-world—the vestibule of the world of light and perfect knowledge. Her remains were, at her request, cremated at Woking, near London, in presence of a considerable number of her and the Society's friends. The ashes were recovered after a brief delay of two hours, and are to be preserved in a silver urn. The London press teemed with articles, mostly of an unkind and personal character, yet all agreeing in the acknowledgment of her personal greatness. The *Birmingham Gazette* of May 12th puts the case thus sententiously: " Mme. Blavatsky was either a woman of most transcendent power with a mission almost divine, or she was the most shameless charlatan of the age ". We, her intimates, do not hesitate to place her in the first category.

" If she were an impostor," says the *B.G.*, " and deliberately an impostor, no words can express the abhorrence with which her impiety and mendacity must be regarded. If she were not an impostor, but 'a messenger from the Masters', the world, as it awakens to the truth, will ever regret that it refused to receive her, and that to the last it ridiculed her doctrines, and suspected her motives. In Mme. Blavatsky's life there is no black spot to be detected by the microscope of the critic. She did good deeds. She preached purity and self-denial. She taught that virtue was excellent for virtue's sake. Her philanthropy was well-known, and her beneficent labours for the East End slaves have been acknowledged and appreciated. So far as personal example could testify, she was a woman worthy of admiration. But the moment her religion was considered, and more specially the means taken to prove its righteousness and its divine inspiration, confidence was shaken."

This is the crux : let posterity judge between her and her detractors.

" No doubt "—continues the same paper—"these people are in sincere belief. We are loth to call Mme. Blavatsky a schemer, a fraud, and an impious romancer. We prefer to think that she laboured under hallucinations, and that in a desire to do great good she was led to trickery, subterfuge, and deceit. It is not wonderful that she obtained a following ; it is only deplorable.

     ✧   ✧   ✧   ✧   ✧   ✧   ✧

" There is only one redeeming feature in the Theosophic movement. It aimed at making man regard his life as precious, and as worthy of purification ; and it endeavoured to lead the human race to regard themselves as one community, united in the great effort to learn their relationship to each other and to their Maker."

We need not quarrel about theological terms, since our critic concedes that we follow aims so noble as those above defined. Only a truculent bigot would deny us this justice.

Our private advices from London relate that letters and telegrams of condolence came pouring in. My experience in Australia and here at Colombo, has been the same. I gratefully thank all friends for their kindness. Our Buddhist schools in Ceylon were closed for two days as a mark of respect, and after my lecture on " Australia ", at Colombo, on the evening of the 12th June, I took promises of subscriptions to the amount of Rs. 500 towards a " Blavatsky Scholarship Fund ", the interest upon which is to be devoted to the support of two Buddhist girls attending our schools. Some thought of putting up memorial tablets, but I considered this the better plan. It is what I myself should prefer, and I am sure she would also. What are grand tablets or statues to this tired pilgrim who has gone out from our sight into the presence of the KNOWERS ? Let her memorial be the golden precepts she has translated from the Mystic Volume. Let the mourning disciple weep—not for her death, but for what she had to suffer in life, in body and soul, unjustly or justly, as her *Prarabdha Karma* may have worked it out. She knew the bitterness and gloom of physical life well enough, often saying to me that her true existence only began when nightly she had put her body to sleep and went out of it to the Masters. I can believe that, from often sitting and watching her from across the table, when she was away from the body, and then when she returned from her soul-flight and resumed occupancy, as one might call it. When she was away the body was like a darkened house, when she was there it was as though the windows were brilliant with lights within. One who has not seen this change, cannot understand why the mystic calls his physical body, a " shadow ".

H.P.B.'s enthusiasm was a quenchless flame at which all our Theosophists lit their torches, an example which stirred the sluggish blood like the sound of a war trumpet.

Finished is thy present work, Lanoo. We shall meet again. Pass on to thy reward.

H. S. Olcott, P.T.S.

What H. P. B. did for me.

MY first introduction to H. P. B. took place at an important meeting of the London Lodge T. S. in Mr. Hood's rooms in Lincoln's Inn, where she suddenly and most unexpectedly made her appearance, having come over at a moment's notice from Paris in obedience to that voice whose commands were ever her absolute law. From the time when I first looked into her eyes, there sprang up within me a feeling of perfect trust and confidence, as in an old and long-tried friend, which never changed or weakened, but rather grew stronger, more vivid, and more imperious as close association taught me to know the outer H. P. Blavatsky better. Not that I could always understand her motives and actions; on the contrary many a night has been spent in pondering, in anxiously seeking a clue—that could not be found. But, however puzzled, I could never look into her eyes without feeling sure that " it was all right somehow ", and again and again the feeling was justified— often months or even years afterwards—when the turning of some corner in the pathway of my own inner growth gave a new and more extended view of the past, and made its meaning so clear and obvious that instinctively the thought rose in the heart, " What a blessed fool I must be not to have seen that ages ago ".

H. P. B., however, was very slow indeed to interfere with anyone's life, to advise or even to throw light upon its tangled skein—in words at least. When we first met, I stood at the parting of two very different life-roads ; repeatedly did I ask her guidance and direction ; well did she know that any words she spoke would be gladly, eagerly followed. But not one hint even could I extract, though she was acquainted in detail with all the facts. Seeing, at last, that I had no right to force upon another the responsibility for my own life—the first lesson she ever taught me—I decided on adopting the course which duty to others seemed to point out. All was settled, every preparation made, trunks and boxes packed for departure to enter on a new line of life. I was in the act of bidding her farewell at midnight; she stopped me with the words, "If you do so and so (*i.e.* follow the course I had decided upon) the consequences will be thus" (*i.e.* disastrous to myself and others). We parted; by morning I had decided to act upon her warning, did so, changed the whole tenour of my life, and stand to-day in my present position. Looking back over the years that have fled since she uttered those few words, I see clearly that her warning would have been fulfilled with the certainty of fate, had I not heeded her voice; and though, since then, my debt of gratitude to her guiding and saving hand has grown like a mountain avalanche, yet I look back to those few minutes as perhaps the most decisive in my life.

But the debt owed to H. P. B. on this and similar scores is small compared with other items in the long account, which even the faithful and devoted service of many lives will fail to balance.

Born with the sceptical and scientific spirit of the closing 19th century, though brought up in the truest sense religiously, thought and study early dissolved away every trace of faith in aught that could not be proved, especially faith in any future such as is taught by creeds and churches. Entering on life with no surer guide than the "constitutional morality" innate and educated into almost every child born of parents such as mine; with a sentimental admiration for altruism and unselfishness drawn from the example and loving care of home surroundings, which the relentless logic of a hopeless materialism was slowly gnawing away; what would have been the probable outcome? Surely a slow descent into utter selfishness and self-absorption. From this fate H. P. B., by her teaching, her experimental demonstration, above all by the force of her daily life, saved me as she saved many another. Before I knew her, life had no ideal worth striving for—to me at least—since the ultimate blank destruction to which material-ism *must* point as the final outcome of the world-process, chilled each generous emotion or effort with the thought of its perfect uselessness; left no motive to strive after the difficult, the remote, since death, the all-devourer, would cut short the thread of life long ere the goal be reached, and even the faint hope of benefitting generations yet to come sank into ashes before the contemplation of the insane, idiotic purposelessness and meaninglessness of the whole struggle.

From this enervating paralysis, crushing all real inner life and tainting each hour of the day, H. P. B. delivered me and others. Do we not owe her more than life?

Yet further. Every thinking or feeling man finds himself surrounded on all sides by terrible problems, sphinxes threatening to devour the very race unless their riddles are solved. We see the best intentioned efforts do harm instead of good; blank darkness closes us in; where shall we look for light? H. P. B. pointed out to us the yet dim star shining down the pathway of time, she taught those who would listen to seek within themselves its ray, pointed out the road to be travelled, indicated its sign posts and dangers, made us realise that he who perseveres and endures in self-forgetting effort to help humanity holds in his hands the clue to life's tangled mazes, for his heart and mind alike grow filled with the wisdom that is born of love and knowledge, purified from all taint of self.

This H. P. B. caused many to *realise;* does she not deserve all our devotion ?

How can I write of my own personal relations with, or feelings towards H. P. B. ? With her in Paris ; constantly seeing her at the Arundales' in London ; at the Gebhards' in Elberfeld ; again in London before her departure for India in the autumn of 1884 ; I took up the thread in Ostend in 1887. Thenceforward working daily and hourly at her side, striving to help, however feebly, in her noble work, I left her only at her express command to go on "foreign service" ; for she never suffered personal affection or feelings to weigh one straw in the balance when the good of the Cause was concerned.

Writing thus after so many have spoken of her, there remains little upon the surface for me to record, and I cannot express aught of the feeling and consciousness that lie below. None but her own equal could ever give a true picture of our leader, whether as loving friend, as wise teacher, as more than mother to us all ; stern and unbending when need arose ; never hesitating to inflict pain or use the surgeon's knife when good could be wrought thereby ; keen-sighted, unerring to detect hidden weakness and lay it bare to the sight of her pupils—not by words, but almost tangibly ; forcing by daily, hourly example whom she loved to rise to the level of her own lofty standard of duty and devotion to Truth ; H. P. B. will ever occupy a unique place in our hearts and minds, a place ever filled with that ideal of human life and duty which found expression in her own actions.

One marked characteristic of her life, both as a whole and in detail, was a marvellous singleness of heart and purpose. She was above all else the Servant of Man ; none came to her with a sincere, honest appeal for help and failed to get it ; no enemy, no one even who had most cruelly and wantonly injured her, ever came to her in need and was thrown back. She would take the clothes off her back, the bread from her mouth, to help her worst, her most malicious foe in distress or suffering. Had the Coulombs ever turned up in London between 1887 and 1891 in distress and misery, she would have taken them in, clothed and fed them. To forgive them she had no need, for anything approaching hatred or the remembrance of personal injury was as far from her nature as Sirius from the earth.

Thus she bore her heavy burden, the Karma of the T.S. and all its members good and bad, in ill-health, physical pain, utter exhaustion of brain and body, working day and night for the Cause to which she had vowed her life. A spectacle this not often to be seen, and more seldom still finding an imitator. Few, but those who enjoyed it, realise how great was the privilege of close association with her in her work; to me it stands as the greatest of boons, and to deserve its resumption at some future time shall be the purpose of my future. Most keenly I feel how little I profited by the grand opportunity in comparison with what might have been gained in power and knowledge to serve humanity; but each of us can assimilate only according to his preparedness, and what lessons we can learn depends on our own fitness, not on the favour of our teacher. Therefore let us strive unceasingly to be better prepared when next that teacher comes amongst us.

Many are the tributes of gratitude, love, and devotion that H. P. B.'s departure has called forth. From circumstances mine comes to stand among the last and briefest; but it is in deeds not words that her life must blossom and bear fruit in her pupils. She left us the charge " to keep the link unbroken ", to hand on to others the help she gave so freely to ourselves. Let us up and be doing, Brothers, for the time is short, the task mighty, and our Teacher's noblest monument will be the growth and spread of the light she brought to the world.

Bertram Keightley, F.T.S.

H. P. B.

(Read at the Convention of the European Section of the T.S., by the Spanish delegate.)

THE Foundress of the Theosophical Society; the Initiate in Divine Wisdom; the noble woman, who with incomparable self-sacrifice and courage, gave up her position, her fortune, her comfort, and even her country, in her love for humanity, for the sake of spreading the Eternal Truth—is dead. The Theosophical Society, which sorrows over this irreparable loss, has just received a terrible blow, and it is not within my power to measure, at present, the consequences entailed by the death of its Teacher on the Society.

My desire is more modest. I wish only to speak of the links which united me to H.P.B., and of the mighty influence which her high-souled individuality exercised upon me, on my method of thought, of feeling, and also on my views of moral, intellectual and material things—in fact on my whole life. I regret indeed being obliged to write from such a personal standpoint, but I think that, perhaps, an analysis of my present moral condition may be useful and analogous to that of many of my brothers here present, who like myself were honoured by the personal acquaintance of H.P.B. It will have, at any rate, one great advantage: that is, my words and experiences are based on personal knowledge, and not on hearsay, and when we are considering moral and even spiritual questions, there is, I think, only one sure criterion—personal experience. In the remarkable article published on the 15th June, in the *Review of Reviews*, Mr. A. P. Sinnett well says: " She dominated every situation in which she was placed, and she had to be either greatly loved or greatly hated by those she came in contact with. She could never be an object of indifference."

Now in my opinion this statement is very correct, and I have no doubt that my brothers here present will agree with me. When first I came to London with the sole aim of meeting and knowing H.P.B., whose gifts had made a profound impression on me, I realised that I was going to make the acquaintance of the most remarkable person of this age : remarkable alike for the depth of her knowledge and for her vast wisdom. It was no mere curiosity, but a feeling of all-powerful attraction which drew me to her, a feeling *sui generis*, which can only be explained on an occult basis. The reality was beyond my utmost expectation ; I felt that the glance of H.P.B. had penetrated and destroyed the personality that I had been up to that moment : a process, new, strange, inexplicable, but most real, effectual and undeniable, was accomplished in the innermost recess of my moral and spiritual nature. The transformation took place, and from that moment the old personality, with its ideas, tendencies, and prejudices more or less ingrained, disappeared. I shall not try to explain this seemingly startling fact, which like all others is based on the great law of Karma ; but never will it be erased from my memory. Every time I saw H.P.B., my affection, loyalty and admiration for her increased. To her I owe all that I know, for both mental tranquillity and moral equilibrium were attained on making her acquaintance. She gave me hope for the future ; she inspired me with her own noble and devoted principles, and transformed my everyday existence by holding up a high ideal of life for attainment ; the ideal being the chief object of the Theosophical Society, *i.e.*, to work for the good and well being of humanity.

Her death was a bitter grief to me, as to all those who are working for the common cause, Theosophy, and who having known her personally, have contracted a debt of undying gratitude towards her.

I have lost my Friend and Teacher, who purified my life, who gave me back my faith in Humanity, and in her admirable example of courage, self-sacrifice, and disinterestedness, and virtue, I shall find the strength and courage necessary for working for that cause which we are all bound to defend.

May her memory be blessed !

These, dear brethren and friends, are the few words which I wished to say to you, greatly desiring to declare before you all that I shall never forget what I owe to H. P. Blavatsky.

Let enemies and materialists explain, if they can, the power and attraction of H.P.B., and if they cannot, let them be silent.

The tree will be known by its fruits, as actions will be judged and valued by their results.

JOSÉ XIFRÉ.

(Translated from the Spanish.)

The Press.

DURING the last month we have simply been inundated with cuttings. Upwards of 500 have been received from Great Britain alone; in fact the whole press of the country has had something to say of H.P.B. and Theosophy. The majority of the cuttings are favourable and many papers re-produced the life of H.P.B. from *Men and Women of the Time*. A few were eulogistic and some had the bad taste to vilify the dead, heaping on her the most shocking imputations. With regard to these the following protest was drawn up and appeared in quite a host of papers:

"We, the undersigned members of the Theosophical Society, who have known intimately the late H. P. Blavatsky, have read with surprise and disgust the extraordinary and baseless falsehoods concerning her life and moral character circulated by a portion of the press.

"We do not propose to attempt any answer in detail to libels as monstrous as they are vile, libels which deal, moreover, with supposed events laid in distant quarters of the world, without any evidence being adduced to substantiate the allegations. Is it right, even for the sake of soiling a dead woman's memory, to ignore the ordinary rule of law that the *onus* of proof lies on the accuser? What character can be safe if any unsupported slander is to be taken for proved fact? We content ourselves with staking our honour and reputation on the statement that her character was of an exceptionally pure and lofty type, that her life was unsullied and her integrity spotless. It is because we know this that we were and are proud to follow her guidance, and we desire to place on public record the fact that we owe to her the noblest inspirations of our lives.

"As regards the curious idea that Madame Blavatsky's death has given rise to any contest for her 'vacant place', will you permit us to say that the organization of the Theosophical Society remains unaffected by her death. In conjunction with Col. H. S. Olcott, the President of the Society, and Mr. William Q. Judge, a prominent New York lawyer, Vice-President and leader of the movement in America, Madame Blavatsky was the founder of the Theosophical Society, and this is a position that cannot well be carried either by a *coup d'état* or otherwise. Madame Blavatsky was Corresponding Secretary of the Society, a purely honorary post, which, under the constitution, it is unnecessary to fill at her decease. During the last six months, in consequence of the growth of the Society, she temporarily exercised the presidential authority in Europe by delegation from Colonel Olcott, in order to facilitate the transaction of business, and with her death the delegation naturally becomes void.

"Her great position in the movement was due to her knowledge, to her ability, to her unswerving loyalty, not to the holding of office; and the external organization remains practically untouched. Her special function was that of teacher, and he or she who would fill her place must have her knowledge.

(Signed) "ANNIE BESANT.
"C. CARTER BLAKE, Doc. Sci.
"HERBERT BURROWS.
"LAURA M. COOPER.
"ISABEL COOPER-OAKLEY.
"ARCHIBALD KEIGHTLEY, M.B. *(Cantab.)*

" G. R. S. MEAD, B.A. *(Cantab.), Sec. European Section T.S.*
" WALTER R. OLD, *Sec. British Section T.S.*
" CONSTANCE, COUNTESS WACHTMEISTER.
" W. WYNN WESTCOTT, M.B. *(Lond.)* "

LONDON, *May 19th, 1891.*

On the whole the newspaper men have shown a desire for fair play ; in fact one prominent journal which had devoted several columns in two succeeding issues to a rehash of the personal opinion that made Mr. Hodgson so notorious, and was so foolishly endorsed by a learned society (perhaps to enliven their otherwise deadly dull reports) sent a representative to visit the Blavatsky Lodge, and gave us an excellent notice in one of its columns.

We have also received many cuttings from the United States, India and the Continent, and have to report on them also as above. It is to be remarked that the press of all these countries, perhaps we may say of the world, has not been contented with a few lines of notice or comment. Many of the leading papers have devoted editorials to the subject, and some contain articles of several columns in length. On the whole, the world imagines that the members of the T.S. are long-haired mystics or credulous imbeciles ; we wonder how they will take it when they find out that we are somewhat business-like people, only a little more in earnest than the majority !

Women's Printing Society, Ltd., Great College Street, Westminster.